WEDNESDAY
& ROCK'n'ROLL

TALES FROM THE EAST BANK

by

Anthony Cronshaw

Second edition published in 2006 by
Juma Print Ltd.
Trafalgar Works
44 Wellington Street
Sheffield S1 4HD
Tel: 0114 272 0915
Fax: 0114 278 6550
Email: juma@btconnect.com

ISBN 1 872204 31 7

Printed by Juma

Acknowledgements

I would like to thank:

My Mum and Dad (Marie and Jim) for looking after me all these years, and my sister and brothers (Donna, Mark and David) for being there. Also my wife's Mum and Dad (Barbara and George) for the past 20 years.

Most of all I thank my wife and daughter (Christine and Samantha) for being my inspiration to write this book.

My many friends who have shared my experiences all these years, and not forgetting **Sheffield Wednesday Football Club** for all the good times.

Tony

iv

Contents

We'll support you evermore 1975 - 1976

The sun was shining through the gap in the curtains right into Tommy's face. It was 6am and time to get up, for today was an important day for Tommy. It was the first game of the season and his beloved Sheffield Wednesday were away to Southend United. Wednesday had just been relegated to the third division of the football league for the first time in their history.

Last night Tommy went out for a drink to the Mill, a disco pub in Mosborough, with three mates Billy, Bob and Chas. The talk all night was about their trip to Southend, into unknown territory because the lads had not been to Southend before. Just before closing time this girl came up to Tommy and said "Fancy coming back to our house? Me mam and dad are away for the week at Skeggy." Tommy thought for a moment and, though the offer was very tempting and she wasn't half decent, the thought of oversleeping and missing the match was too much of a risk to take. Anyway he thought she would probably be in the Mill on Sunday night, so if the offer was still on for Sunday and he overslept he would only miss work.

Tommy was now ready and headed for the meeting point, which was at their local the Royal. The rest of the party were already there. Billy, Bob and Chas from last night, Trevor who had known Tommy from school, Gaz who was a couple of years younger, Archie who had arranged the trip, Rich and Shess who were the same age as Bob, and Mick and Chris who were the old men of the group.

The bus turned up on time and the boys set off at 8am, which would give them plenty of time to reach their destination. Then disaster struck. As the bus was on the M1 just before the A617 to Mansfield the bus started to slow down. It limped off the motorway and headed for Clay Cross finally resting on a garage forecourt. Archie was having words with the driver who told him that a replacement bus was on its way. As the boys sat around feeling sorry for themselves, Tommy chirped up "It's all right for you lot, but I could have been in bed with that bird from the Mill." So Shess replied, "Well fuck off then!" Finally at 10.30am the replacement arrived and off they set. Now it would be touch and go whether they would make the kick off.

The driver really put his foot down and by 2.30pm they were just entering Southend. The boys legged it out of the bus and made their way to the turnstiles. It looked as if all the blue half of Sheffield had turned up. It was a glorious sunny day and Tommy thought to himself this is the only way to watch football and not piss wet through, stood on the East Bank at Hillsborough.

The game was a drab affair, probably because the Owls were beaten 2-1, "But never mind" commented Billy, "Let's hit the town and have a few beers!" When the boys got back to the bus the driver said "Come on lads. If I get my foot down we will be back in Sheffield for 9 o'clock." Archie then informed the man that the bus was booked to return from Southend at midnight. "Oh shit!" Was his reply "I'm supposed to be taking our lass out tonight when I get back?" "You'll have to phone her and say you'll be a bit late," laughed Chas. So the boys headed for the sea front and the first job was to get something to eat. They settled on a fish and chip shop on the sea front. When they had filled their empty stomachs with a good portion of fish and chips it was time to finish the evening off with a few pints. The boys headed for a pub on the seafront called The Foresters. By the time the boys got in it was full of 'Wednesdayites'. A band was on stage doing the best they could under the circumstances. But as you know when football fans get together and you mix it with drink its time to party. The band was now fighting a losing battle to be heard over the din that hundreds of beer swilling football fans could make. Tommy said to Bob "Fancy going for a walk, because if I carry on drinking at this rate I'll be on my arse by 9 o'clock?" Bob agreed and they left the others in the pub and made their way out into the evening sunshine.

As they walked across the road crowds started to gather each side of the promenade. Bob asked this old dear what was happening. She said "It's the Southend Carnival Parade." All they could see in the distance was loads of floats making their way down the seafront. Just then Tommy heard raised voices behind him. It was some chap in a navy blue uniform telling the old folks they couldn't have a deckchair because all the chairs had to be away by 7pm. As Southend's answer to Hitler had neatly stacked all his chairs away and headed off into the sunset leaving all the old dears of Southend stood on their pins, Tommy said to Bob "we will now do our good deed for the day and make a few bob in the process." As the attendant buggered off Tommy set about dismantling the neatly stacked pile of chairs, passing them onto Bob who handed them to the grateful public, who handed over whatever small change they had. There was no set fee for this service but anything would be appreciated. Just as the boys were in full swing the before-mentioned deckchair attendant returned and challenged the boys "What's going on here?" He shouted Tommy replied, "We're doing your job so fuck off!" This he promptly did shouting "I'll be back with a copper." This was the cue for a swift exit and back to the safe haven of the Foresters. As they were crossing the road a Wednesday fan ran to the float carrying the carnival queen and proceeded to let off a fire extinguisher in the girl's direction. The poor girl was covered in a white wet foamy mess. She was hysterical and so were hundreds of onlookers.

As the fuss died down the boys entered the pub and sat quietly in a corner. Bob emptied his pocket where he had put the change from the hire of the deckchairs. The sum total was £3.80, not bad for ten minutes work! By this time the rest of the boys were well oiled and in a bit of a state. Outside the pub now was a large number of the Southend Constabulary who were trying to contain the supporters to a small section of the seafront. The lads decided to try their luck and find another pub away from the mass of coppers. After walking away from the front for ten minutes they found a cosy little drinking hole just outside the town centre. By this time Tommy's body was quickly filling up with beer, but his pockets were quickly emptying of cash. Never mind, he thought, if he did finish up skint he could tap Billy who always had a wad of money on him.

The time was now getting on and the boys supped up and left the pub. In the end it was a bit too quiet but, as they made their way back to the front, the noise from the direction of the seafront seemed to be getting louder. When the lads walked around the corner just outside the Foresters the Police were starting to make arrests. Now in all the confusion the said officers would sometimes make mistakes and it was not unusual for the innocent to be singled out and thrown into the back of the Black Maria, so you had to have your wits about you or it could be a court appearance first thing Monday morning, after spending the rest of the weekend as guests of Her Majesty. It's then up before the beak, a fine in excess of fifty quid and allowed to make your own way home, probably sometime Monday afternoon. Now, as most supporters don't budget for the eventuality of getting collared, not many carry enough to get home on that Monday afternoon. As train fares are out of the reach of most fans, it could turn out to be a bit of a nightmare getting back to Sheffield from, say, Southend.

By this time the lads had been separated from each other in the confusion, Tommy found himself with Bob, Billy and Chas. The coppers were getting really on top and after getting abuse for the last five hours they were not to be reasoned with. As the boys ran back in the direction of where the minibus was parked, Tommy was thinking to himself that he hoped none of his party had been wrongly picked out, as not only would it be an inconvenience to the said lad but also the rest would be delayed for their return home. When the boys got back to the bus nobody was missing.

The time now was just after midnight and with a bit of luck they would be home by five in the morning. As they were driving through the night back to Sheffield Tommy thought to himself what a day this had been, and it was just the start of the brand new season. But then again he felt in his pocket and pulled out the vast amount of 75p. That's all he had left and he thought to himself "Bloody expensive game being a football fan." The bus pulled up outside the Royal at 5.30am and the very tired bunch emerged, said their goodbyes and went their separate ways. Tommy and Bob lived in the same direction and as they were walking home, Bob said he could not wait for the next away game, which would be against Darlington on Tuesday night. Tommy replied he could not wait to get into bed as he was knackered. They both said what a great time they'd had and went their separate ways. As Tommy lay in bed he thought to himself what would this first season in the third division bring and with that thought he dropped to sleep.

Next morning Tommy was awoken by his brother Mick, "Waste of time that was going down there to watch that crap and spending all your money. Well don't tap me cos I ain't got anything to lend." "Doesn't matter" replied Tommy, "Dad will give it me cos he's a Wednesdayite like me, not a fucking Blade like you." Then in walked the youngest of the three brothers, Danny. He was only eight, but had the ability to make money even in his sleep. Not only did he help Mick with his paper round but often would spend hours on the local golf course retrieving lost golf balls and selling them on at a small charge. Often during the school holidays he would never be seen from early in the morning until it was time for tea. So Tommy knew that there would not be a problem getting the money together for the match at Darlington, because if his dad didn't have it, Danny would.

Mum then shouted them all as it was time for Sunday dinner. This was the only time that all the family would sit together for a meal, because dad worked shifts and would work mornings, afternoons and nights. This sometimes caused a problem for Tom because mum had a part time job working in a city centre pub. She only worked Friday and Saturday nights, but if the lads were on the piss celebrating anything and it fell when dad was on nights, Tommy would have to give it a miss. This was a slight inconvenience sometimes but it was only one night every so often.

Dad took Tommy to his first Wednesday game in March 1964 when they were playing Arsenal at Hillsborough. The game ended in a 4-0 defeat for the Owls but Tommy was hooked, and with living in nearby Southey, Tommy was allowed to go on his own. So from that day Tommy would go once a fortnight to see the Owls.

In the year 1966 Wednesday went on their famous cup run reaching the final of the F.A. Cup but, unfortunately for

Tommy, every game was played away. Then came the draw for the semi final; Wednesday would play Chelsea at Villa Park on the 23rd of April 1966. This would stick with Tommy forever.

About three weeks before the game Uncle Don came to see Tommy's dad. "We are going to Villa Park fancy coming?" "Definitely" was the reply. Now Uncle Don said to Tommy, "Seeing that we will be working can you get the tickets for the match? You will need to get eight." As Wednesday were only allocating two per person, Tommy would need help if he was to get all eight tickets. He dragged his best mate Chris along with him and they started to queue at about 5.30am.

As the queue was getting longer Tommy wondered, why didn't he drag along another two and it would all be over first time round. But he didn't and after the first time round and with four tickets safely in his pocket it was a mad dash to the back of the queue to start the process all over again. By this time Tommy and Chris were getting really tired, and they never thought they would ever reach the front. At about 4.30pm and nearly twelve hours in the queue Tommy and Chris had achieved their objective. They ran home to be greeted by Uncle Don who rewarded the boys with ten bob each. Now, for two ten year olds, that was a lot of dosh.

On the morning of the match Tommy was so excited that he was going to his very first away game and it was the semi final of the F.A. Cup. He'd been telling all his mates at school he was going to Villa. Now the house was getting fuller and fuller with people Tommy had never seen before. At this point Uncle Don arrived and said to Tommy "All the lads want to thank you for getting them the tickets and to show our gratitude we have bought you this case ball." Tommy's eyes started to fill up and he blubbered "So I'm not going?" to this

his dad replied "Whatever gave you that idea?" and at that point Tommy ran from the house across the road to Grandma's.

Now, Gran was not one to be messed with and Tommy told her the whole story, only pausing to wipe away the tears. Grandma stormed across to see Uncle Don and said "Why aren't you taking the lad?" to this Dad replied "We're stopping out late and we'll be going for a drink so Tommy can't go." At that point Gran gave them all a piece of her mind and slammed the door behind her nearly taking it off the hinges. As she entered her house Tommy was still sobbing. "Now look here, stop that crying and listen!" Said Gran, "They are all going to the match with their mates from work, when you get older you will realise why they can't take you with them." At this point Gran explained "Next season Granddad will take you to watch Wednesday if they play away in the F.A. Cup." On hearing his name mentioned Granddad shot up in the chair, "So where am I taking the lad?" was his reply. "Nowhere," said Gran, "He will have forgot about it come next year."

Oh how wrong could she have been? The following season Wednesday were drawn away to Chelsea in the F.A.Cup and, on hearing this news, Tommy ran to Gran's and said "Me and my Granddad are going to Stamford Bridge to watch Wednesday." On returning home from work Granddad was met with the news that he was going to London to watch the Owls. "Am I buggers?" was his reply. "Now look here," said Gran, "He was let down last year and I am not having the lad let down again, even if I have to take him myself." Now Granddad was not one for football. He was more likely to be found in the King's Head on Saturday afternoons than at Hillsborough.

But Granddad was true to his word and, come the day of the game, he and Tommy were off to London on the train and, as he worked for the railways, he got cheap travel. They got to the ground well before kick off and, with Granddad not being the world's greatest football fan, found themselves on the Shed where all the home supporters congregated. The young lad was overawed with it all. It was nearly a full house and the noise was incredible. As for the game, Wednesday lost 1-0 to a goal in the 90th minute by Baldwin. But the journey home was brilliant. Granddad bought him the biggest bag of peanuts he'd ever seen and by the time he'd finished them the carriage was full of shells and, deep down, I think Granddad enjoyed himself.

During Sunday dinner the subject of Wednesday's game at Darlington came up. Tommy knew that it would be touch and go whether he had the money to fund two away trips in one week. If he hadn't then he could tap his dad, but money was in short supply and he was one in a family of six. The youngest, Debbie, at the age of six was not really into football. Anyway he could always rely on Billy. He knew that if all else failed Billy would come up trumps.

On the day of the game the boys met in the Claymore at 2.30pm. They had all finished work early. Only Tommy, Billy and Bob were going. Chas and the rest could not get time off work. The lads had booked with the S.U.T. as they didn't like going with the supporters club, because they were always slagging off the fans that sometimes would get into a bit of trouble. The buses were to set off at 3.30pm and with a bit of luck the boys would get a couple of pints before the game.

On the way to Darlington the topic of conversation was Saturday's trip to Southend. Tommy said "Did you see the star on Monday night? All the trouble made the front page." He added that his dad was not impressed about the behaviour of the Wednesday supporters. Billy added, "I don't know what all the fuss is about. According to the paper there were only seven arrests. I bet there's more in town any Saturday night." And with that bit of useful information he slumped back into his seat. They arrived at the ground around 6.30pm, just enough time for a pint, if they could find a pub.

The lads made their way into the ground just after seven. Tommy looked around but could not see any friendly faces and wondered if or how many Wednesday fans were in the home section. This was to become apparent when the teams took to the field. A shout went up to Tommy's right "Wednesday, Wednesday..." was the chant. At this signal all hell broke loose; people were stumbling around the terracing like a heard of wildebeests not knowing which way to turn. At this point, Tommy felt a blow to the side of the head, which sent him flying down the terracing and coming to rest against the perimeter wall. Fists and boots were flying everywhere and, in the fracas, Tommy was trying to get back on his feet. At this point a gap was opening up between the two rival sets of supporters and, in no-mans-land, the police were starting to take control. This was Tommy's signal to return to the section of Owls fans that numbered about 50.

Things started to calm down for a short while and only the odd insult was exchanged across no-mans-land. This was soon to change because the Owls scored. All the hostilities were forgotten as Wednesday were actually winning. Everybody was leaping about hugging, kissing and fondling each other. Why were the fans doing this, grown men acting like six-year-olds in the school playground? This was Darlington's signal to attack their rivals who were off-guard, forgetting that only ten yards away were a bunch of like-minded fans who wanted to do the boys some serious damage.

The police had either temporarily lost it, or else some officer decided that because Wednesday were in the home section they were fare game. The battling 50 stood their ground and the boys were really enjoying it. Little Bob was like a maniac.

Peace was soon restored with the officers once again taking control and yet again the unbelievable happened: Wednesday made it 2-0, "Have I died and gone to Wednesday Heaven?" shouted Billy, what a night. "The Owls had actually won away from home and I've seen it" thought Tommy.

Outside the ground all the trouble was forgotten as they made their way back to the coach. Tommy was surrounded with so many happy smiling faces, this was what being a football fan was all about. For the next three hours all the supporters would be on a high.

Back on the bus Tommy took his seat and in front of Tom were two men discussing the evening's match. One said "What a result" to which the other replied "Yes, but it was spoilt by those so-called supporters who are giving the club a bad name." "They're not even true supporters" replied the other. This made Tommy's blood boil. Everybody is entitled to their opinion, but when they questioned his loyalty to the Owls, Tommy flipped. "Who are you to question my fucking loyalty to the club? Just because I sometimes get into a spot of bother it doesn't make me a lesser fan than you two! At this point Billy pulled him back into his seat and told him to shut up. "I've got to be at work for 4am so I need some kip."

The bus pulled into Pond Street just after midnight so the boys ran to the station to get a taxi. "Can you pay my fare?" asked Tommy. To this Billy replied "And I suppose you're skint an all Bob." Bob just nodded. The taxi dropped them outside the Royal and, as the boys made their way home, Bob said "We've had quite a couple of days haven't we?" To this Tommy replied "Yes, not only am I completely knackered, but so are my pockets. I'll have to tap our Danny to get to work in morning."

As Tommy slumped into bed he glanced at the clock. "Oh shit!" he thought. "I've got to be at work in seven hours. It's a tough life being a football supporter" and at that point he nodded off.

Two more league games were to be played in August, resulting in a 3-3 draw with Brighton and defeat at Hereford. Also by the 3rd of September Wednesday were out of the League Cup, going out to Darlington on penalties after losing the home leg 2-0, resulting in a third game which ended 0-0. Darlington won 5-3 on penalties.

By the time the boys were getting ready to visit Chesterfield the Owls had picked up only five points out of a possible twelve. It was not a good time to be a Wednesdayite!

On the evening of the game the lads met in town straight after work. British Rail were laying on a soccer special, when they transport as many fans on one train and pack them in like sardines. Billy was not very happy after paying good money to find himself crammed in a carriage with what seemed like hundreds. "No wonder there's fucking trouble when they herd you in like cattle" he said. Bob replied "Well, at least we won't be on for long, as the journey to Chesterfield should only take 20 minutes." As they reached their destination the boys quickly made their way to the ground. It was now 6.45pm and the queue for the Wednesday end was massive. We'll never get in for kick off at this rate said Chas.

Anyway, just after 7, the lads made it into the ground. In the home section fighting broke out between the rival supporters, and a small group of Wednesday fans had infiltrated the home section. Being out-numbered and getting pushed against the perimeter wall, the Owls were up against it. This led to a pitch invasion from the opposite end of the ground. The Wednesday fans from the away end were charging across the pitch, the boys included. Like the seventh cavalry going to the rescue, Tommy was sprinting across the pitch, his heart pounding as he made the dash to the Chesterfield end. The sight of hundreds of Sheffielders heading towards them made some home supporters leg it out of the way as the boys teemed into the home section and pockets of fighting broke out all over the place. The Wednesday fans that were outnumbered earlier now had the numbers on their side and retaliated against their original aggressors. The police were now wading in to restore order and a gap was opening up between the rival supporters. Tommy had lost his mates in the melee that followed. As the match kicked off the rivals were taunting one another across no-mans-land. The police were wading in and making arrests from both sides. Tommy had to have his wits about him so made his way to the side furthest away from the police. He'd had his fun and exchanged a few blows with the opposition, but did not want his collar felt, thus spoiling an enjoyable evening.

The match ended in yet another defeat for the Owls. Outside the ground the boys made their way towards the Railway Station. The thousands that had made the short trip to Saltergate were rushing to get on the first available train to Sheffield. As they made their approach to the Station the lads could see in the distance Wednesday fans going crazy and smashing anything they could get their hands on; windows were being put through, cars vandalised and total mayhem was erupting. This did not go down too well with the boys, as they could not see the sense in mindless vandalism. When all was said and done what pleasure can you get from putting a brick through a window?

Tommy did not like this sort of behaviour from the Wednesday fans. Not only did he find it pointless, but knew when his dad read about it he was going to get grief, even though he was not involved. As the lads got to the station it was a mad scramble to get on the train. They were packed in like cattle but, lucky for them, it was only a short journey back to Sheffield.

Once back at Midland Station they were met by hundreds of coppers who looked a bit pissed-off to say the least. The lads quickly made their way out of the station and into Pond Street to catch the last bus home. When Tommy finally made it home the family were still up. Dad said "Lost again have they?" even though he had not known the result. Mum chirped up "It's about time you started saving your money instead of wasting it watching that load of rubbish." She added "Why can't you save at least some of your money like Michael. He's never skint like you and he doesn't even earn as much as you." Tommy, as much as he loved his mum, could not stand it when she went on and on, always saying Michael does this and young Danny does that. It really did his head in and with that bit of information still ringing in his ears he went to bed.

As Tommy got into work the next day the talk was all about the exploits the night before. The Unitedites taking the piss after the Owls had lost again, and the lads giving it back to them, stating that most of the Blades that worked with Tommy, the nearest they got to the Lane on a Saturday was when their old lass would send them shopping down the market for the week's groceries. The foreman chirped up that he hated work the next day after Wednesday or United had played because nobody did any work. They were all too busy slagging one another off.

The season was now in full swing and the Owls were struggling, picking up only another eleven points up to Christmas. The highlight being a 4-1 thrashing of Millwall at Hillsborough on the 11th of October. On the day of the game the lads knew that the boys from London had quite a bit of a reputation and would bring a few to Sheffield. The lads met at the usual time to catch the bus to Hillsborough and, with a bit of luck, they would be in the club at the ground for 12.30pm. The club was quite popular with the home supporters and it was always packed, so you needed to be early to get a seat. The lads were all sat having a drink when, at about 1.30pm, someone ran in and said that Millwall were on the East Bank. Everybody jumped to their feet, supped up their ale and made for the Kop. This was time to have a crack at the infamous F-Troop. Millwall were right at the top of the Kop and were in a good position, tightly grouped with their backs to the railings. Whoever was in charge of this lot knew exactly what they were doing. By the time the lads got in the Wednesdayites were congregating under the electric scoreboard, just milling around, not quite not knowing what to do.

The boys from London had the upper hand, even though they were now getting out-numbered. The only way to get at them was to charge up the steps from either side. As the Owls fans were getting into position to attack, the Millwall supporters went for it, realising that they were now getting heavily out-numbered everybody was going at it hammer and tongues. Tommy was really loving this trading blows with the infamous F-Troop and ragging one or two of them about, sending them hurtling down the East Bank. At this point the Millwall supporters were heading for the safety of the pitch. The lucky ones who had a head start made it on to the pitch in time, those stragglers at the back were taking a bit of a beating. Once onto the pitch they were taunting the Wednesday fans to follow. The police were now out in numbers and it seemed pointless to pursue the enemy any further. But you'd got to hand it to the Lions from the Den as they were as game as anything Tommy had ever seen.

The lad's next trip was the Boxing Day trip to Bury and they were all going. A bloke they knew called Webbo had a

Transit van and, for the right money, would take them anywhere. So on the morning of the game the lads crammed into the Tranny and set off to Bury, hoping that the van would not breakdown and get them there for opening time. There must have been thousands making the short journey across the Pennines and everyone was in a festive mood. Tommy was loaded because he was not back at work until the 5th of January 1976, and he had got three weeks' money which would probable be spent by the end of the week!

When the teams came out it was like Wednesday were at home. One fan was on the pitch jigging about and kicking in with the players. The coppers didn't seem to mind and there was not one hint of trouble. It was if everybody was here to party with it being Christmas. Shess decided to join the fun on the pitch, but he was that pissed he fell over his own feet and went crashing into the penalty area. When he returned to the terracing he was as black as the ace of spades. "What your lot laughing at?" he spluttered, wiping the mud off his brand new sweater that probably his mother had bought him for Christmas.

The game ended in a 0-0 draw so at least the Owls had not lost. When the boys got back to the van it was freezing and, as they set off back to Sheffield, Chas wanted to know if they were stopping off on the way back for a drink. "Why?" was the reply. "Because I'm supposed to be meeting this bird at 8 o'clock." The boy should have kept his gob shut because now everybody else would want to stop for a drink just to wind him up.

Anyway he arrived back in plenty of time and the boys finished off the evening in the Royal. As they sat round the table Billy wanted to know who was going to Charlton in the F.A. Cup on the 3rd of January, because the S.U.T. were running a bus that was stopping in London until midnight and that, on the way to the home game against Mansfield tomorrow, they would book. Billy, Tommy and Bob were definitely going. Also going was Eric who didn't go as much as the others, but the thought of a night out in London appealed to him.

On the morning of the game in London the lads met in Pond Street in the café to have a cup of tea and a greasy bacon sandwich to send them on their way. Tommy's mum had packed him some sandwiches, but he kept that quiet from the rest of the boys, not because he was greedy, but he didn't want them taking the piss. Billy hated the long journeys, but with a bit of luck they would be in London for dinnertime.

As the coach reached the ground it was quite apparent that the Owls had brought a fair following. The boys made their way to the nearest watering hole and set about making the most of their day out in London. After sinking one or two pints they made their way to the ground, going into the section marked visitors. This was a fun day out so getting involved with any trouble was put to one side. There was a good following from Sheffield behind the goal.

As the teams came out, fighting broke out to the left of Tommy and Wednesday fans were running from where the fighting was taking place. Tommy couldn't understand this as Charlton did not have a reputation for causing grief. As the boys were moving towards where the fighting was it was quite clear that this was not Charlton, but was those infamous boys from the Den who had come especially to have another go at the Owls.

"Millwall, Millwall..." was the cry as the Owls were trying to regroup, and fists and boots were flying. Tommy was trying to get a piece of the action but was taking his time as he didn't want to get too close and get dragged into the mass of Millwall thugs. He chose to wait until one would become separated from the pack. Just at this point he saw his chance as one had broke ranks and stood there arms outstretched beckoning his rivals. His eyes were filled with hate and Tommy could feel them burning into his face. Tommy flew at him and gave him a clout to the side of the head. He swung his fist catching Tom in the mouth drawing blood. Tommy landed another beauty that unbalanced the boy and, as Tommy waded in, another Wednesday fan booted the Cockney in the head, sending him sprawling on all fours. The boy disappeared under a sea of boots and fists and Tommy was none too pleased that his battle had been taken over when he had the upper hand.

The terrace was in total mayhem. Millwall started to retreat, not that they had bottled it, but they were totally outnumbered. Those in the Wednesday ranks that had first legged it were now coming back for a piece of the action now that the Lions were in retreat. Tommy retreated back to watch the match as he found no fun in chasing a retreating set of supporters across the terracing who were quite clearly outnumbered.

The match finished in a 2-1 defeat for the Owls. Outside the ground all hell broke loose and exactly what happened at Chesterfield was happening again; mindless vandalism, cars were being smashed and overturned, even houses were having their windows put through. This was well out of order and Tommy, still sporting his cut lip, was totally pissed-off. This is not what it is all about, mindless destruction of people's property. Finally they got back to the coach and headed for the drop-off point at Victoria Station. Now finally to end the evening with a bit of fun in London and no trouble, the boys found a bar just around the corner from the station and settled down to spend the next six hours sinking a few beers and having a laugh. As the boys were chatting Tommy was still messing about with his cut lip. "Will you leave that alone?"

shouted Billy. "Anybody would think you'd been fucking twelve rounds with Henry Cooper and not been smacked by some southern softie." Tommy proceeded to sip his beer and trying to avoid opening up the cut. Just then Bob noticed two birds sat at the bar with long flowing hair and wearing long fur coats. Bob fancied his chances with those two. "I think I'm going to chat them up" he said. "Well as soon as thy opens thi gob tha's blown it" replied Eric. As he got to his feet and walked towards them Billy said "I bet he's back with us in two minutes flat." Bob said "Excuse me" to the two women. As they turned to face him his face was a picture. "Yes Love" replied one. "Sorry mate but could you tell us where we can find a decent boozer?" "Yes try the Golden Lion just round the corner. They have a singer on every Saturday night." With this piece of useful information Bob scurried back to his seat. "Sup up," Shouted Bob "We're off." As the boys finished their drinks and were leaving, Tommy took one last look at the two women at the bar and could not believe his eyes. "It's two blokes" he shouted. "I didn't know tha fancied fellows Bob." "Bollocks" he replied. "And that's what you'd have got if you'd have copped off with one of them. Two big hairy ones" laughed Tommy.

The lads made their way to the Golden Lion where the singer was in full swing blasting out the current classics. He was totally murdering Bohemian Rhapsody by Queen. This upset Bob because they were his favourite band. Tommy was more into Roxy Music and David Bowie, but enjoyed any kind of music.

The lads spent the rest of the evening touring the pubs and bars around the area, bumping into the odd Geordie who had also been in London that day watching Newcastle United. The atmosphere was really civilised between the two sets of supporters from up North. The lads finished off the evening with the Geordie boys.

The coach left bang on midnight for the journey home, Tommy sporting his cut lip, Bob still pissed off with his encounter with those two puffs, Eric was worse for wear as he can really knock them back, 'a real beer monster,' and finally Billy who was fast asleep. Tommy finally got home just before six on Sunday morning. As he slumped into bed and thinking what a good time they'd had, he thought to himself "I've got to get another job that pays more money because I'm always skint, and with that thought dropped off to sleep."

By the 31st of January the Owls had got a massive total of 19 points. The record was W4 D8 L8 F26 A29 and on the 17th of January the lads arranged with Webbo to take them to Grimsby. "Who's going? he asked. "About a dozen" replied Tommy. "We need to be in Cleethorpes for 12 noon" said Bob.

"There's bound to be trouble today" said the boys as they jumped into the back of the van. It was only a couple of hours to the seaside, but that was in normal modes of transport and not in Webbo's Tranny. "The next person who takes the piss out of my van can get out and walk" chirped Webbo. Today he had his mate with him, Frank. He was a real nutter in his forties. This, thought Tommy, was an added bonus in case they bumped into any trouble before the game.

The lads arrived at Cleethorpes on time as Webbo's van had come up trumps. The place was packed with Wednesday fans and all the pubs that were open were doing a roaring trade. It was not the best time of year to visit the East Coast as it was bloody freezing. The lads spent the rest of the time having a few beers before moving to the ground. They had decided to leave the van in Cleethorpes and walk to the ground as Webbo didn't want to pull up outside the game and have over a dozen blokes jump out of his Transit in full view of the Police.

The game finished in a 1-1 draw with Rodger Wylde scoring the Wednesday goal. After the game the party of fourteen made the long walk back to Cleethorpes. It was quite dark now and the boys were being followed by some unfamiliar faces. "Keep close together," said Billy, "I think were going to have some bovver with this lot." Tommy could not make out who was who and this made the situation uneasy. He thought to himself with most of the coaches parked in the other direction, the Wednesday fans heading in this direction would be minimal.

As the lads approached the roundabout that led to the town centre Billy said "Lets go down this side street and see if they follow, and if they do we turn and face them before we get too far down the road." As the boys made the left turn off the main road Billy was right, they were Grimsby and the boys were outnumbered. They had two options: they could leg it and run for the van, or they could turn and have a go. Tommy said "What do you think?" To this old Webbo replied "Well I ain't running." The boys knew that the lads that were with them would not run and stick together and they had the added bonus of Mad Frank. Billy said "Let's turn and see what they do" and at this point the boys turned to face their aggressors. For a split second the Grimsby boys stood still before charging at the boys. Fists were flying and the lads were holding their own and I think Frank was really enjoying himself. Webbo was like a man mountain and I don't think anyone was going near him!

The Grimsby boys were now getting on top and the lads were losing big style. All of a sudden this big guy at the front of the Grimsby supporters shouted to his gang to back off. Tommy could not understand it, why the opposition had gone off like they did when the boys were truly beaten. Not that he was complaining because the lads looked a sorry sight, except for Webbo, and Frank. As they walked the last hundred yards to the van Billy was wiping his bloody nose, Bob was not too bad, Tommy had got another thick lip, Shess and Mick seemed too be all right, Chas was limping, Gaz, Trev and Chris were o.k. but Ian, Archie and Young Ray seemed to have come off worse.

They looked a sorry sight when they got back to the Royal. The landlord said "I thought you were going to a football match. If that's what you come back like I'm glad I like Cricket. The boys finished the evening off with a few more drinks and Tommy said "I'm going to get cleaned up and have an early night" and with that he left the rest and headed home. How was he going to explain his face over the Sunday dinner table? He knew dad would give him grief and that mum would be tut tutting all afternoon, but that was tomorrow and, in the meantime, he needed some kip.

Tommy got through Sunday lunch quite unscathed and finished off the weekend as usual with the rest of the lads at the Sunday night disco at the Harrow. Tommy really liked Sunday nights because the boys would take in their own drinks. They would take it turns beforehand to buy a bottle of gin or vodka. Tommy's favourite was Bacardi, but the rest were not too keen on this. Anyway the boys would buy half a beer or lager and then spend the rest of the evening giving the spirits a right seeing to, with just the odd visit back to the bar for a bitter lemon or coke. The evening always seemed to finish just as the boys were in full swing. The lights would come on and everybody would sup up and depart into the night.

Tommy was up bright and early Monday morning and off he went to work. On clocking in, Tommy was surprised that there was not the usual banter coming from the canteen.

As he walked through the door he was greeted with deadly silence. "What's up with you lot? Somebody died?" Tommy joked. "Yes" was the reply from old Dennis, "The firm is shutting down." "Oh shit" Tommy said. "Yes, we have been told that the place will close at the end of February leaving us all out of a job." This was not the news Tommy wanted to hear. What would he do? He had been here since leaving school. He knew the money was crap but it took him to football and bought his beer. It was not like going to work. It was a pleasure to turn up everyday because everybody just had a laugh, but they did graft so he could not understand why it wasn't making any money. Mr Shaw, who owned the place, addressed all the workers at dinnertime and told them that the place was too small and that his major customers were importing their furniture from Europe and so he'd decided to call it a day and close the factory at the end of February.

Tommy was really upset, not just for himself but that most of the older chaps would find it difficult to find another job. At the end of the day Tommy set off home to break the news to his mother. As he walked through the door mum was busy preparing the tea. "Get yourself a cuppa," mum said. "It's just mashed." "Mum," Tommy said, "I've got something to tell you." "Yes, what is it?" she replied. "I'll be out of a job at the end of next month. Mr Shaw is closing down the factory." "What are you going to do?" she asked. "I've not got a clue," said Tom. The rest of that month was a disaster; not only did Tommy not know what he was going to do, but Wednesday were still struggling to get away from the bottom of the league.

The fateful day came on Friday 20th of February 1976. Mr Shaw took all the workers to the pub at dinnertime and told them that, to show his appreciation, the drinks were free all afternoon. At first Tommy thought that he would get legless but, on second thought's, he didn't want to go home in a right state and get an ear bashing from mum. So he decided to just have a few to be sociable. Most of the lads were in no mood for celebrating, to the landlord's dismay. The rest of that weekend Tommy stayed in, only to go to Hillsborough to see the Owls beat Aldershot 3-1. He knew that mum would be advising him to budget accordingly, but how could he follow the Owls on his dole money?

Monday morning he went to sign on for the first time and after he had filled in all the forms the lady showed Tommy a list of vacancies that she thought he would have a good chance of getting. After viewing them all Tommy did not fancy any of them. "I can arrange an interview if you like. In fact this one, which I think suits you the best, I can ring him now and you can see him this afternoon." Blimey, Tommy thought the ink was not even dry on his forms and this woman was trying to fix him up with a job as though her life depended on it. Tommy kindly informed the lady that the job did not suit him because the said firm worked all day Saturday. "Is that a problem?" she asked. Tommy thought to himself before giving his answer. "Yes, it is quite a big problem. You see I go to football on Saturdays so taking that job was out of the question." Once Tommy had exhausted every avenue that she was trying to lead him down, I think she gave up on him and told him that he should sign on every Tuesday at 10am. Deep down I think she wanted to say every Saturday at 3pm.

After leaving the dole centre he made his way home and, on reaching the house, his mother was just having her dinner. "Any luck?" she asked. "No" said Tommy. This ritual was to be repeated day in and day out, right through to the middle of March.

By the 17th of March the Owls had picked up another 7 points bringing the grand total for the season to 26.

The next big game for the Owls was the local derby away to Rotherham United. On the morning of the game the boys met as usual outside their local and were going to the game by public transport, thus avoiding the massive police presence at the railway stations in Sheffield and Rotherham. The boys got to town quite early so decided to stop at the greasy café in Pond Street to get a bite to eat. Shess said "It's going be a long day of football, fighting and boozing." When the happy bunch had finally got their fill of culinary delights they made their way to catch the bus that would take them straight to Rotherham town centre.

The bus was quite full with like minded souls who were looking to frequent one of Rotherham's finest drinking holes before the match. Finally, on reaching the town centre, the boys headed for the Turf Tavern because Tommy once worked with some guys from Rotherham and would sometimes go out with them for a drink. Once inside the Turf the boys headed for the bar only to be told that they were not serving groups of lads that came in together unless they were known to the bar staff. So, with the chance of getting a drink in here rather slim, the boys moved up the stairs and out onto the street. "What we going to do now," asked Gaz. Billy replied "Find a pub that will serve us!"

Shess suggested that the boys split up into smaller groups so having a better chance of getting a drink. At this rate the lads would be stone cold sober by 3 o'clock. Tommy said "Look, lets try the Red Lion. It's a much quieter pub than the rest so lets trickle in, in ones and twos. They headed for the Lion which was not far from the Turf. Once inside the boys sat quietly in the corner doing what they do best - drinking and talking football. The pub was a mix of people who had been shopping and had stopped far a swift one before carrying on their journey home. The old men sat in the corner playing dominoes and not a hint of trouble. "Shit in here!" commented Young Ray. Isn't there any where in this Shit-hole with a bit of life?" Tommy was a bit pissed off with Ray's remarks as he had only been coming with them since the Grimsby game and he was always moaning about this and that, but deep down Tommy respected him for the way the youngster stood his ground at Grimsby.

After another couple of beers the lads took Ray's advice and went looking for a more livelier pub. This they found when they entered the Dickens pub. This was a big boozer that was popular seven days a week. It was quite full with what you might call 'a fare mix' of football supporters. It was still early and there was still over one and a half hours to kick off.

Then everything kicked off with a small skirmish to the far side of the pub involving no more than a dozen chaps. Then it soon erupted into a full-scale ruck. At first it was hard to distinguish who was who because nobody wore colours. The boys formed a tight-knit group so as to protect themselves from anyone who got too close. Shess realised that the small mob in the corner were Rotherham and, like a madman, he somehow broke rank and charged at the enemy with fists flying like some kind of demented windmill. The boys quickly followed him, not wanting him to get all the glory. The boys were quickly on top and the roles were reversed. From the encounter at Grimsby they were calling the shots.

Just then another group came in from behind the lads and this lot were tooled up with bottles and chairs. This was getting out of control. It's one thing to have a good set too with fists and feet, but to start using weapons like this in a confined space was well out of order. Everybody was now spilling out onto the street and into the middle of the road. The Rotherham fans were mostly in the pub except for the odd ones that had been dragged outside. The Wednesdayites that were now outside were attacking the pub with anything they could lay their hands on. In Tommy eyes this was not the done thing but those scumbags deserved all they got.

Now that the police were on the scene the lads decided to complete the trio of activities for the day and go and watch a game of football. Some of the group were up for going on the Tivoli end, but others were not so sure. They'd had a good day so far and felt it unnecessary to show bravado by going in with the opposition. Anyway, Tommy wanted to watch the game, so it was left to the individual to decide which side of the ground they would go in. Most of the boys decided to watch the game but Young Ray, Ian and Shess plumped for the Tivoli. As the boys got into the ground there was fighting on the Tivoli end with the police finding it difficult to keep the rival supporters apart. Fans were getting ejected from the ground by the dozen.

During the game, that was a drab affair, things did calm down a little until those tossers from Rotherham scored. "I can't believe it, getting beat by that fucking load of shite" Billy said, while they made their way to the Railway Station looking rather rejected. As the boys piled on to the train they were herded in like cattle. The lads managed to get a compartment all to themselves with the exception of Young Ray who was missing. The train had just pulled out of the station when it came to a sudden stop. Someone had pulled the emergency cord bringing proceedings to a stop.

All manner of activities were taking place. The fans were going mad, smashing everything in sight. Just then this young lad burst into the compartment clutching a fire extinguisher, "And what are you gonna do with that?" said Bob. "Put it through the window." was the reply. "Well if tha does you'll be fucking following it, so fuck off." To this the lad sent the object flying out of the next carriage window. The train had now started to move off but had not got far when the cord went again. Billy looked at his watch. It was now five to six and the train had not even reached the Tinsley Viaduct. Shess was getting really mad now it had been nearly four hours since he had his last drink. Finally the train pulled into the Midland Station just before seven. The journey that should have taken fifteen minutes took over an hour and half.

The coppers were out in force and when the boys emerged from the train they could see why. It was smashed to pieces, except for the place where the boys were sitting. One young fan was laughing as he left the train and the police grabbed him and marched him off. The boys made their way out of the Station and into Pond Street to get the bus to the Harrow, the boys' favourite drinking hole of a weekend, where they had a disco on most evenings.

The boys placed themselves in their usual position near the door. The topic of conversation was the game, the fight, the train journey home and oh, I wonder what happened to Young Ray. At about ten o'clock he walked in the door. "Where's thy been?" was the question. To this he replied that after the game he had gone into the town centre to have a drink and, for the past five hours, had been chased round Rotherham town centre by some right nutters. Finally he'd ended up walking to Tinsley to get the bus to Sheffield. I don't think they took too kindly to us invading their poxy town. Last orders were now being called so it was time for one more beer then off to the chippy to finish the day off in style with chips, fishcake and curry sauce.

The rest of March saw Wednesday take only two more points giving them this amazing record of W8 D14 L16 giving a grand total of 30 points. So the month of April was going to be crucial if the Owls were to stay up.

The last eight games of the season saw the Owls win four times beating Crystal Palace, Bury and Halifax and taking a point off Shrewsbury and only losing to Wrexham and Mansfield Town. Now we come to the final two games of the season.

First it was the away game at Brighton and Tommy was totally skint. The lads were deciding who was going as there was not enough to take Webbo's van. Come to think of it would it make it to the south coast? Billy could not go anyway as he had a wedding to go to, Shess and Mick did not fancy it because the beer was shite. Chas, Ian and Young Ray plumped for the Supporters club because it was cheap. But this was still too expensive for Tommy. Then Bob had an idea, "Let's hitchhike down to the game, Tommy." Tommy thought that was the only option so the boys put their idea into action. The boys asked Frank if he could take them down to Nottingham with him on Friday.

On Friday morning Tommy packed a bag with some warm clothes because they would be sleeping rough tonight. He also had made some sandwiches, but these were only to be eaten when they were really starving because he could not see them returning home before Sunday night. He called round for Bob and they set off to meet Frank. As Frank pulled up and they got into the cab he told them that they must be mad to spend three days sleeping rough just to watch a game of football. They just nodded in agreement with him.

Frank dropped them off just outside Nottingham where they waited on the slip road of the M1 motorway. Bob had made a sign which read LONDON on one side and BRIGHTON on the other. Just then a big lorry pulled up and as Bob opened the door the driver asked "Where abouts in London do you want to be?" "Any road that will take us to Brighton" was Bob's reply. The driver just laughed and said "You lucky bastards. I'm going eight miles outside Brighton cos I live in Shoreham," and that was the only time Tommy was glad to hear that name mentioned. The driver said that the journey would take about six hours with all the stops he had to take.

His first stop was on the services at Watford Gap where he stopped for something to eat. He asked the lads if they wanted anything to eat but they replied "Only a cup of tea" even though they were both starving. Once back on the road the driver asked Bob why they were going to Brighton. "To watch the football." "I didn't know Brighton were playing tonight" he said. "No, they're not. It's tomorrow afternoon." said Tommy. "Who do you support then?" he asked. "Sheffield Wednesday" was the boys' reply. "I'm a Palace man myself" said the driver. The man was now throwing the wagon round the narrow streets of London as though he was driving a little mini.

Once they had got to the other side of London they stopped again. Once inside the roadside café the driver asked the lads if they would like something to eat and, even though they were famished, the boys said they were O.K. To this the driver replied, "I know I am hungry and I've already eaten once today, so I suggest you swallow that northern pride and pick anything from the menu." Up shot Bob and Tommy and made their way to the counter where Tommy ordered Chips and Steakpie, four slices of bread and a large tea. "Make that two luv," said Bob. As the boys tucked into the plateful of grub as if there was no tomorrow the driver was chuckling to himself. "What's funny?" said Bob. "You two" said the driver. "If your not hungry then I don't know what is." The lads had had their fill and it was nearly 5 o'clock when they were dropped off. They thanked the driver for his kindness and made their way across the road to stand under the flyover.

It had just started to rain when this car pulled up. As the boys bent down to talk to the driver they noticed that he was a man of the cloth. "Where are you going?" the vicar asked. "Oh, just into Brighton sir" Tommy replied. As they jumped in the car and sped off towards the town it was now raining heavily. "I just came along in the nick of time" the vicar said. "What brings you to Brighton?" he enquired. "Oh were going to the match tomorrow" replied Bob. "Where are you staying tonight then lads? the vicar asked. "We'd probably get bed and breakfast somewhere" was the reply. As the vicar dropped the boys off on the sea front they thanked him for the lift and said their goodbyes.

It was now nearly six o'clock so they headed for the nearest café to get a drink. "Two teas please" Tommy asked the girl behind the counter. "That will be 30p, thank you." the girl said. "Robbing get," Tommy muttered as he returned to his seat. The boys made the teas last forever before finally the stares were biting into the backs of their necks. The boys got up and walked out into the cool night air. They had budgeted so that they could afford two pints that night, so the boys just wondered round the streets aimlessly for the next couple of hours just killing time.

It was now just after nine so the boys went in search of a quiet boozer so that they could kill off the next couple of hours in peace. "I have never took so long to sup two pints of beer" said Tommy, thinking back to the first game of the season when they were downing them for fun. Bob said "Come on, sup up. Lets find a chippie. I'm starving." The boys found a chip shop and quickly joined the queue. When Bob got to the front of the queue he asked the woman serving, "Chips and Fishcake wrapped with plenty of salt and vinegar on please." You should have seen the heads turn to marvel at these two strange creatures from another planet.

Once outside Bob handed one package to Tommy and the boys wandered off in search of somewhere to doss down for the night. The boys walked through a large park and came across a cricket pavilion. "This will do." said Bob, looking for a way in. Around the back someone had left a window slightly so Bob managed to lift the catch and the boys climbed in. Snuggling up to one another to keep warm they opened their supper. "Shit." cried Tommy. It's a bleeding rissole not a fishcake." Bob was soon to discover that he too had got a stinking soggy rissole. "Don't they now how to do a proper fishcake these Southern morons?"

The boys soon finished off their supper and settled down to get some kip. "Don't forget to shut that window and check if all the doors are locked. We don't want any visitors during the night." The boys had quickly made the place secure and were soon in the land of nod.

They awoke about six the next morning gathered all their belongings together, even the empty chip papers, and made their exit the same way as they got in. It was now still eight hours until kick off, so the boys headed for the sea just to kill some time. First on the agenda was a public convenience so they could freshen up. They found one just by the multi story car park. Once inside the boys did the best they could to liven themselves up. A quick brush of the teeth, a quick rinse and back out onto the streets. Tommy said "Let's go and get a cuppa, I'm gagging." So off they set in search of a café.

Once the boys had left the café they went onto the beach where a group of lads were playing football. As the boys got closer they could recognize the accent. "Where you lot from?" asked Tommy. "Worksop" came the reply. Tommy and Bob introduced themselves to the Worksop Owls. "How you got down then?" Bob asked. "In our Kevin's Transit" was the reply. Tommy then asked if they could fit them in for the journey home. The young lad ran to ask the rest of the group about Tommy's proposal. "No problem" came the reply. What a godsend that was, not having to worry about the return journey.

The boys packed up the game and headed for the Tranny. Kevin opened it up and Tommy and Bob threw in their bags. "Did you see the mattresses in the back?" asked Bob to Tommy. "Sure did" was his reply. It was now opening time so the boys hit the boozer. They now had a bit more money to spend than before due to getting the lift home. The boys spent the next couple of hours chatting to their new found friends. It was now 2.30 and time for the match.

On reaching the turnstiles there was such a commotion from the front of the queue. Then this copper came up to the lads and said that no one could come into the ground wearing heavy working boots or Doc Martins unless they handed in the laces first. "I've never heard such a load of crap in all my life" said Tommy. "Don't they know that a football hooligan can do more damage with a good stiff pair of brogues than any pair of bovver boots?" Bob removed his laces and put them in his pocket. Once inside he sat on the terracing and set about the task of re-threading his laces.

The teams came out to a tremendous reception from both sets of supporters. Tommy and Bob were on the side terracing but some Wednesday fans were in the home section. This led to a few scuffles breaking out but nothing major. The rest of the game passed off peacefully but, by the end of the match, the Owls had come away with a credible 1-1 draw.

Once outside the ground trouble was breaking out all over the place. Tommy and Bob got separated in all the commotion that was going on. Tommy found himself down a side street with a small group of Owls fans. He was finding it hard to get his bearings on which direction the Transit was parked. Just then a group of Brighton fans came into the street. Tommy was unsure how his new found friends would react.

"What shall we do?" one asked. "See what they are made of" said another and with that the group ran at the Brighton supporters and the Southern softies legged it. Now, Tommy's main objective was to locate the Transit and hopefully Bob. As Tommy rounded the corner the Tranny was standing there. Delightful thought Tom, no worries about getting home. Just then the Worksop lads appeared. "Where's your mate then?" one asked. "I don't know" said Tommy. "I lost him straight after the match." "Well we will give him ten more minutes then we'll have to be off." Tommy pondered oh shit. On one hand he couldn't go with out him and on the other the Transit looked so inviting. But it only took a minute for Tommy to reply. He said "If he's not back then I'll have to wait for him. Pass me the bags out lads" Tommy asked.

Just then who should come running up the hill? It was Bob. "Where's thy been?" Tommy wanted to know. "Well we got into this fight and before I knew it I was on the seafront having a right old battle. It was tremendous. Wednesday had them all over the place. It was funny really. We had this big skinhead legging it and his boots were flopping all over the place cos he'd got no laces in." The group jumped in the Transit and off they set. It was really comfy in the back laid on the mattress. They were not long out of Brighton when the pair were fast a sleep. The Worksop lads pulled off the M1 at the junction with the A57 that led to Worksop in one direction and Sheffield in the other. The boys jumped out of the Tranny and thanked them for the lift.

It was now 10 o'clock and the boys had quite a walk home. As they trudged their way through Swallownest they were really knackered. Only Beighton and Hackenthorpe to go then they were home. As the pair walked through Beighton it was chucking out time and the streets were full of drunken yobs and, as the lads were unfamiliar with the surroundings, they needed to be careful as they didn't want any hassle so near to home. Just then four youths came in the opposite direction. "Just keep walking" Tommy said to Bob. As they walked passed the youths one said "Where you two off to then?" "Home" replied Bob. "Where's tha been then" said another. "Match" replied Tommy. "Bit late to be coming back from Lane in it? they said. "Not been to Lane, been to Brighton mate" said Tom. "A Wednesdayite is no mate of mine" said the gobshite one. "Let's have em" they shouted. Tommy didn't want this but was too knackered to run. As the two battled gamely against the odds, two blokes came out of the Cumberland pub and came to the boys' rescue. Now the tide had turned and the aggressors were soon on their bikes. "You two O.K.?" said one. "Yeah, not bad mate" "What was that all about then?" said the other. "We've been to Brighton and got dropped off at motorway and are walking home when they took objection to us being Wednesday fans." Tommy and Bob thanked the two who also happened to be Blades and carried on their journey. By now they were knackered and Bob said "That's it, I'm phoning me Dad. I'm not walking another step." Within 20 minutes Bob's dad had picked them up and by midnight the boys were both in bed. Tommy lay there touching yet again his bruised lips and thinking to himself that he needs to find a job before the new season because he is fed up with always being skint, and with that thought dropped off. Now for the final game of the 1975-76 season...

Ironically, where it all started back in August, the opposition was Southend United, but this time they were coming to the temple of the gods better known as Hillsborough. Well over 25,000 were to attend this crucial game for the Owls including all the boys who had seen it start back in August. Everybody was really tense as the game got under way as defeat today would probably send the Owls into

35

the fourth division, and what a nightmare that would be. Tommy found the atmosphere electric and it reminded him of that dreadful night when the Owls lost to Manchester City and were relegated out of the first division. This time, however, it was to all end happily ever after with the Owls victoriously winning 2-1 thanks to goals by Prendergast and Potts, so bringing to a close the season 1975-76. But what would be waiting round the corner when Tommy and the boys were to see it all start again in the month of August 1976?

East Bank Republican Army (We're Barmy)

Wherever we go, we fear no foe,
cos we are the E.B.R.A!

1976 - 1977

After spending most of the summer looking for a job
Tommy finally found one, through a friend of his dad's called
Colin. Colin owed Tommy a favour because he was one of the
buggers who pissed off to Villa Park in 1966 leaving Tom at
home sobbing. "You start first thing Monday morning at six"
his dad said. "Six in the morning? What sort of time is that?"
he replied. It was an engineering firm down Attercliffe, so
Tommy would have to get two buses to work. "I'll have to be
up by 4.30 every morning" he thought. "Well at least they
don't work Saturday's and that's a good thing." Tommy's job
was keeping the machine shop tidy, emptying the lathes,
unloading the steel off the lorries and, most importantly,
fetching the chips at dinner.

On his first morning at work he arrived at about 5.30. He
was well early, dad would be proud. An old man called Arthur
would show him the ropes this first week because he was
retiring on Friday. Arthur had been with the firm since 1950
since coming out of the army after the war. Tommy respected
the old man for sorting out those German Bastards and for
serving King and Country so well. He listened to everything
Arthur told him because he needed to have it all sorted come
next Monday. Friday came and everybody went to the Dog and

Partridge to say a fond farewell to old Arthur. It wasn't so bad his first week, even though he had to be up at that ungodly hour. What was also good about the job was that they all finished at noon on a Friday. Tommy stayed until chucking out time as he had got quite friendly with two of the apprentice machinists. One was a Blade called Brian, the other was a 16 year old called Chris who was a Wednesdayite. "Going to the match tomorrow?" the young lad asked. "Never miss" replied Tommy. "Are you going?" Tommy asked the young lad. "Yes, I'm going with me dad. We're both members of the supporters club." Tommy thought bastard, it's Grimsby away in the League Cup and Webbo's taking the Transit. So he thought that if there's trouble and the lads are in the thick of it, as usual, that's going to be a fine start Monday morning if young Chris spots Tommy acting up.

In the Royal on Friday Bob was finding out who was going to the game so he could tell Webbo the numbers. It would be the lads who went to Southend twelve months ago, plus Ian, and not forgetting Young Ray. They were to leave for the game later than last year because Webbo had a job to do and could not pick them up until dinner, which didn't give much time for a drink before the game. The remainder of the evening was just spent locally and the boys finished up in the Harrow before setting off down town. Just before closing Alan walked in looking for old Joe. He had been fishing and brought the old man some eels. "Let's have a look" asked Bob. To this Alan took them into the toilets and emptied the eels into the sink. Old Joe was not in so the boys decided to grab one each and head off down town.

Tony was the first to offload his when he asked the chip shop owner for chips and eel. "We don't sell eel" came the reply. "Well fry us this fucker then." Tony shouted and proceeded to throw the eel in the fryer. The man went mad,

"You've contaminated all my food. Get out, you're all barred." The fun, and all the eels, were nearly gone as the boys entered the Daisy. Tommy had still got his left but it was making a mess off his hands.

Tommy waited for the opportunity to dispose of the eel and it came straight away. A lad had just put his pint down to go for a piss and Tommy was in like a shot. He carefully slipped the eel into the lad's beer and then waited for him to return. The lad picked up his pint with the handle and took a swig. He had not disturbed the creature lying at the bottom of his drink. At the next mouthful the pot was dispatched out of his hand and onto the floor leaving the offending eel heading in the direction of some women, who were not impressed with the lads actions to say the least, and had thought he had thrown it at them. The poor lad was ejected out of the club along with the slimy eel.

The boys finished the evening off in hysterics and downed a few more beers. Webbo picked them up and set off for the East Coast. "There won't be time for a drink before the game but we can stop off on the way home if that's all right with you Webbo" said Bob. So the lads went straight into the ground before the game. The Owls had brought a large following. There were the odd scuffles but nothing to get excited about. Wednesday played really well winning the match 3-0. Tommy was really pleased with the start to this new season. "Brilliant wern't we?" he told the lads, as the boys headed back to the van. They did not encounter any trouble at all, to Young Ray's disappointment. "Don't worry Ray, it's only the start of a long hard season" said Bob. Billy commented that with the likes of Rotherham, Chesterfield, Lincoln, York, and another trip to Grimsby we'll have plenty of opportunities to find trouble. Bob finished off the conversation saying that Portsmouth, Crystal Palace and Brighton would give us the excuse to head South and party.

The boys decided to head straight home and aim for the Harrow, the local watering hole. It was quite full when the boys got back, and they went straight to the bar. It was always Soul on a Saturday night and the girls were busy sprinkling talc on the dance floor. "They make me laugh" said Tommy. "They know that we always spill the beer on it and turn it to sludge" he laughed. By 10.30 the boys were off to the Fairway and with it being, technically, in Derbyshire it served until 11 o'clock.

With the time well on the way to midnight it was time to finish the evening off at the chip shop. Sat on the wall outside the lads were all looking forward to this new season. "I hope we have a better time result wise this year" said Billy. "So do we" said the rest. It was time to head home and with Tommy going to a family get together tomorrow that was the end of his weekend. The next few games of the season saw the Owls progress to the next round of the league cup at the expense of Grimsby. They beat Northampton and drew with Walsall at Hillsborough.

Saturday the 28th of August the boys headed off to Port Vale in the back of Webbo's van. "I can't believe that we've crammed in here like sardines" commented Ray. "The reason we use the van is that it is convenient, cheap and we stop for a drink when we want one. I know it's not very comfortable but it serves the purpose and also it's got a nice toolbox" said Shess.

On reaching the ground the boys knew that Vale would be up for it so they headed for the home section. They made their way inside in small numbers, and would always congregate to the left hand side, as close to the back as they could, but not standing together, as a large crowd of unfamiliar faces would bring the opposition onto them before they were ready. Tom stood on his own glancing round to see if he could spot any other likeminded Wednesdayites. He noticed one or two but not many and the Vale fans had congregated as usual behind the goal, surging backwards and forwards in unison.

As Port Vale took to the field and their fans were chanting it was now time to show their presence and "Wednesday, Wednesday..." went the cry. A small band of Blues had grouped together at the top of the Kop and it was Vale's job to come and get them. Tommy's heart was beating like a drum. As they moved from the middle to get closer to the boys you could tell who were the fighters and who were the 'I'm all right at the back' boys. The boys got in close together and charged at the Vale. The boots and fists were flying and a big gap had opened up on the terrace. As usual Young Ray was in the thick of things.

The boys had enjoyed themselves and it was now time to bid the Vale farewell and, slowly, the lads headed towards the pitch. They had overstayed their welcome and it was now time to join the mass throngs of Wednesdayites at the other end of the ground. This was the most dangerous time. Not only did the boys all have to avoid getting separated, but they had to avoid getting nicked. Worst of all was being left stranded on the opposition's Kop on your own and at the mercy of any Tom, Dick or Harry. The boys made their way round the perimeter of the pitch and jumped into the safe haven of the fellow Owls.

The match unfortunately saw Wednesday's first defeat of the season. On the way home the boys stopped off in Buxton for a quiet drink. Webbo said "You can have two hours here. I want to be off by eight." The lads found a nice little boozer and all the talk was about the exploits on the terrace. Tommy thought it had gone quite well and that nobody had been hurt

41

or lifted by the coppers. Bob added that Tuesday night would be a sterner test away to the Wolves in the league cup. If we stick together like we always do then we should be O.K. Webbo said it was time to be off, so they jumped into the bus and off they went. Tommy spent the rest of the weekend in the pub, but needed to save some money for Tuesday. At work Monday morning Tommy was sat having his break when Chris, the apprentice, came up to him saying "Saw you at the match on Saturday with your mates." "When was that?" answered Tom "You were all coming off the end where the home fans were." "We got on there by mistake," replied Tom. The young lad was having none of it. He knew that Tommy was a hooligan, and that he wanted some of the action as well. "Can I go with you to the next game? It's boring with my dad." Tommy was not too keen to have the lad join the lads on match days but he was nearly seventeen. If there was a war on he would be old enough to get killed so Tommy said "Look, you can't come to Wolves because the coach is already full but we're off to Wrexham with Charlie's Coaches in September, so I'll get the boys to book you on." The boy now left Tommy alone to finish his snap.

Tommy finished work early on Tuesday so he could meet the lads in Town for a beer before they set off to Wolves. The bus was leaving Pond Street at 4.30 so after coming out of the pub they still had time to spare so they headed for the bookies. Tommy had a 10p round robin on the next three races. The first was called Orient Boy which obliged at 3 to 1, next up was Welsh Blossom that came in at 6 to 1, and finally the aptly named Within The Law that had odds of 4 to 1. "Over £25 for £1" said Tommy.

The boys headed for the bus and Tommy was feeling very pleased with himself. "Fancy getting a round robin up especially with me being skint" said Tom. "Tha's always was a jammy bastard" replied Shess. Once on the bus the lads settled down for their short journey to Wolverhampton. It did not take long before they had reached the ground. "Which end are we on" asked Ray. "The section behind the goal marked Visitors" replied Tommy.

Inside the ground Wednesday had brought a large following, which was quite pleasing because Wolves could be a naughty place sometimes. With the game coming to a close, and with the score at 1-1, a miracle happened. Rodger Wylde hit the back of the net to make it 2-1 to the Owls. Wednesday hung on to the lead to claim victory. Then all hell broke loose. The boys were so busy celebrating that they'd not noticed the ground empty and the Wolves were heading in the boys' direction. Because the gates were open the Wolves fans were pouring into the Wednesday section. With such a varied mix of supporters it was hard to get organised, but on the other hand all those pouring in had only one thing on their minds, seeking revenge against Wednesday for the fact they had won. The boys grouped themselves together and engaged the irate mob. Totally outnumbered the lads were taking a bit of a hiding.

Fortunately for the boys the coppers came in to restore order. The Wolves fans were herded off the terrace and out into the dark streets of Wolverhampton. Tommy said "We need to stick together and make our way back to the coach." "Thank fuck we've not come in the van and had it parked down some dinghy back street," replied Bob. The boys made their way back to the coach and Tommy was sporting another thick lip for his troubles. Finally the group reached the safety of the coach. "We're not cut of it yet," said Chas. "Keep away from the windows" he added.

The rest of the journey home passed off without incident. The boys could not believe it. They'd dumped the mighty Wolves out of the league cup. On returning to Sheffield,

Tommy asked if anybody fancied going to Daisy. "Not me, I've got to be at work at four" said Billy. Bob said he was up for it, so were Shess, Ray, Mick and Gaz. Tommy's winnings were burning a hole in his pocket, and he couldn't believe he had so much money on him on a Tuesday night.

It had turned three when Tommy arrived home. He didn't feel like work but Dad was on mornings so he had no chance of lying in bed. He had just got to sleep when Dad shouted him, so up he got, bleary eyed, and off he went to work.

Wednesday were now playing well and the lads couldn't believe that, by the end of September, they had seen the Owls win four times. It was now Saturday the 25th of September and the lads were off to Wrexham, with a new addition to the group. "This is Chris lads, he work's with me" said Tommy. The boys were having a drink in the Lion, waiting for the coach to take them to Wrexham. Bob had got friendly with the regulars in the Lion and managed to get them booked on this trip. It was the third trip they had run this season, and if the numbers held up they would run one to all the away games.

Barry, the lad who ran the coach, charged about 50p more than the National Express, so the cost to Wrexham was £2.50. With the added bonus of getting picked up from a boozer this was a right find for the boys, not having to trail into Pond Street every time. Bob had booked for sixteen, which was quite a good turn out. Along with the usual bunch was the added selection of Chris from Tommy's work and three mates of Ray's, who were Terry, Jimmy and Les. It was slow going with Charlies Coaches and it was 2.30 by the time they reached the ground. The boys did their usual trick and headed for the home section where they were met by a large group of coppers. "Where you from lads?" this copper enquired. "Wrexham," answered Tommy "all of us" he went on. "I don't think so" said the jolly policeman. With their plans in disarray the boys trooped off to go into the away end, and watched the game in peace. The game ended in a 2-2 draw thus giving the Owls a grand total of seven points from the first seven games.

It was now October and the Owls were off to Lincoln. This time the lads were going on the Soccer Special kindly laid on by British Rail. The fare for this trip was only £1.80 and they thought it great value for money as it got them to Lincoln by 1 o'clock. The first job was to avoid the coppers and find a pub. This they did and settled down to have a few beers. Ray said that they needed somewhere a bit more lively and Shess countered this by telling him that it would be lively enough once inside the ground.

The lads moved on towards the ground and split into smaller groups. On reaching Sincel Bank they headed for the Home section which was situated behind one goal with the majority of Owls fans congregated on the side of the ground. Tommy paid his money and stood to the front of the terrace reading the programme. This, he thought, would pass on a bit of time until all the others were in the ground. The time now was nearly ten to three and a large group of Lincoln supporters were heading in his direction. They were heading for a small section of supporters who were congregated to the left hand side of the terrace. They stood out a mile. They were Owls fans but were just milling about doing nothing.

Tommy tagged along at the rear of the bunch as he knew that when it kicked off he could throw a few punches from within the group. This was a dangerous thing to do, not only could he be set upon by the home fans, but in the event of the Owls getting the upper hand he could be singled out by them. Tommy noticed some familiar faces to the top of the terrace that he knew would be in the thick of it.

As Lincoln homed in on the fans grouped in the corner, the boys from the top charged in sending most of the home fans heading for the safety of the pitch. Those were the anorak and scarf brigade who didn't get involved in any unsavoury behaviour, and rightly so. It was not everybody's cup of tea. Tommy let fly with a beauty to this kids face drawing blood. Everyone was at it now, even the decoys who had drawn the Lincoln into the trap. Wednesday fans were coming from everywhere to attack the Lincoln. Also the rest of the terrace were charging across to back up their mates who were taking a bit of a bashing.

The Owls were heavily outnumbered and it would be a fight to get out in one piece. Wednesday were getting separated into small groups and Tommy started to make his way to the pitch. Most of the fans were on the pitch side when Tommy tried to get over the wall, only to be dragged back onto the terrace. As he lay with all the empty Bovril containers and pie wrappers, Lincoln were really putting in the boot. Just when all seemed lost the coppers came in and broke up the fun. Tommy explained to the Police that the supporters had mistaken him for a Wednesday supporter and, as he was trying to get out of the way, they had dragged him back into the terrace and attacked him. As the Policeman escorted him to the St Johns, Tommy told the officer that he was all right and he just wanted to go home. "Where do you live?" asked the PC. "Torksey" replied Tom. "So if you don't mind I'd like to go home" and with that Tommy scarpered out of sight of the officer and round to the side where the Wednesday fans were situated.

It was now twenty past three and the game was well under way and, to cap it all, it started to piss it down. Once inside Tommy tried to locate the rest of the boys. This was proving a difficult task with the crowd Wednesday had brought. It was now half time and Tommy located most of his pals. "Where's thy fucking been?" asked Billy. "I thought you'd been nicked" said Gaz. Tommy told the lads how the Lincoln had kicked him about a bit, and that he had told the Police that they had mistaken him for a Wednesday fan and he told them he was from Torksey. "Where did you get that fucker from?" asked Bob. "Me Dad used to take me fishing there and it was the first thing that came into my head" replied Tommy.

The game ended in a 1-1 draw and, as the fans made their way out of the ground, it was now raining cats and dogs. This really put a stop to anymore activity because rain and football violence don't mix.

The train was due back in Sheffield at 6.30, so the boys decided to spend the rest of Saturday night in town. On leaving the station the first port of call was the chippie in Pond Street to get some grub inside them. Having feasted on chips, cake and curry sauce it was time to go to the Claymore for some Newcastle Brown. Tommy liked a couple of bottles of an evening, but it was expensive. Next port of call was the Old Blue Bell in High Street, followed by the Brown Bear, the Stonehouse, the Golden Ball, the Saddle, and finally coming to rest in the West Street Hotel. Some of the boys wanted to finish the evening off in the Daisy, but with a home game on Tuesday night Tommy, Bob, Billy and Gaz decided to take last bus out of Pond Street.

The rest of October saw the Owls make steady progress beating Chester, Gillingham and Reading, but came unstuck against Shrewsbury and Mansfield Town. On the 27th of October Wednesday were away to Millwall in the league cup. The lads had organised a minibus to take them to London. Chas thought it was a bit steep, having to pay £6 each. The idea was to set off early and have a full day in London. They were on their way by 8am, and made steady progress towards the Capital. They arrived in London around dinner time and the driver told the lads that he would drop them at Waterloo Station. "That's fine" said the lads. The driver had arranged to pick them back up at 6pm and take them to the Den. Tommy commented that it was bad enough coming to Millwall on a Saturday, never mind a cold Wednesday night in October. "I don't know what you're worried about. They're only lads like us" replied Shess. "I know but we're on their patch this time and there will be thousands of them" explained Chas.

The boys spent the rest of the day having a few beers, a laugh and games of pool. At 5.45pm the lads made their way back to Waterloo Station to be picked up by the minibus. The time now was getting on and still with no sign of the bloody bus, the lads started to panic a bit. "He'll have to fucking turn up soon or we'll miss the match" said Bob. The time now was 6.45pm and still no sign of the bus. Just when they thought all was lost the bus arrived. "Where's tha fuckin been?" shouted Shess. "Sorry about this lads but the traffic in London is bloody murder" replied the driver. The boys jumped on board and headed for the ground.

While driving down the Old Kent Road the driver spotted a minibus parked under the railway bridge. He pulled up behind the bus and told the boys to be back here straight after the game. It was now 7.20pm, and the lads dashed towards the ground. They just made it in time for the kick-off. They were situated behind one goal, penned in the corner. The atmosphere was very intimidating. Missiles were thrown towards the Wednesday section and this included golf balls, coins, and even lumps of wood. "This is unbelievable" shouted Bob "They're like fuckin animals" added Terry. The match was now pushed to the back of the lads' minds. The main concern now was to see out the remainder of the game in one piece.

48

The final whistle could not have come soon enough for the lads and the Owls had been beaten 3-0. As they made their way out of the ground and back in the direction of the minibus, the coaches that had brought the majority of the Wednesday fans were being stoned and the windows were being smashed. Tommy was walking back to the bus with Bob and Ray and, as they approached the bus, a gang of youths were milling around. Bob said "Just keep walking and don't stop." As the three drew level with the gang one of them appeared to aim something in Ray's direction. Ray fell to the floor clutching his face. There was nothing the other two could do for their mate. Bob disappeared under a sea of boots and fists. Tommy ran into the middle of the road swiftly pursued by the rest of the gang. Tom managed to vault the barrier that ran the length of the Old Kent Road and ran away from the pursuing mob. The cockneys were shouting "Get the northern bastards."

As Tommy reached a gap in the barrier he made for a pub he had spotted on the other side of the road. He ran inside quickly followed by one of the gang. The lad picked up a pool ball and Tommy thought this would be heading in his direction. Crouching he covered his head awaiting the impact.

Suddenly he heard, in a broad cockney accent, "Put that fackin ball down you twat," followed by the crack of a pool cue that descended on to the lad's head. Dropping the ball he picked himself up and made a quick exit. The big pot bellied cockney in a white shirt and braces picked up the ball and asked his mate where it had been on the table. The man quickly deposited the ball back on the table and carried on as if nothing had happened. The landlord came over and ushered Tommy through the bar and into the back yard. He told the lad that if he went out this way he could make his way back towards the ground.

As the landlord opened the back door Tommy looked out onto the most uninviting housing estate he'd ever encountered. Declining the landlord's invitation Tommy went back inside the pub and ordered a pint of beer. Tommy was still shaking as he downed his pint of beer. When he had finished off the pint he peered out into the road. There seemed to be no one around so he steadily made his way back in the direction of the minibus. A police officer enquired if Tommy was from Sheffield. "Yes I am" was Tommy's reply. The officer told Tommy that the rest of his party were in the pub across the road. Tommy entered the pub to be met by all the lads minus Ray. "Where's Ray?" asked Tommy. He was told that the lad and the driver of the other minibus had been taken to Guys Hospital and that now he was here, they could get off to see if he was all right.

On reaching the hospital, the boys were told by a doctor that Ray had been squirted in the eyes by a diluted solution of ammonia. The nurses were cleansing his eyes to get rid of most of the solution. "Bastards" shouted Tom, "Why can't they be content with giving us a good kicking? There's no need to start throwing chemicals about" he added. It was now 2am and they were still seeing to Ray. Then the doctor came out and told the lads that they could do no more for Ray and that they had got most of the ammonia out. "You'll have to put these drops in his eyes every half an hour. "Two drops in each eye" said the doc. Ray came out and his eyes were a right mess. The lads helped him to the bus and off they set. It was going to be a long journey home, having to stop to give Ray his drops.

Eventually the weary travellers made it back to Sheffield at 9am that Thursday morning. All the boys were on a downer with what had happened to Ray. None of them had managed work and Billy, Bob and Shess had gone with Ray to the

Hallamshire Hospital. The rest of the boys were in the pub waiting for the lads to report back on Ray's condition. About 2.45 the boys came through the door with Ray following on. "Well what's the verdict?" asked the boys. "Well my eyes should make a full recovery in time but I'm still going to be an ugly bastard" joked Ray. The boys sat around discussing the cowardly behaviour of the cockney bastards. "It is well out of order using weapons of any kind" they said.

The next couple of months took its toll on the group. Nobody got excited about the fact that the Owls were having their best season for years. By the 18th of December Wednesday had amassed a grand total of 23 points compared to the 14 they had achieved the previous season. It was fast approaching Christmas and the Owls had two games over the festive period. The first being on the 27th at Hillsborough against York City. Over 22,000 saw the Owls win 3-2. The following day the lads got Webbo organised to take them to Grimsby. They set off later than usual because who in their right mind wants to spend Christmas on the East Coast. The boys saw the Owls grab a point in a 1-1 draw and quickly returned to Sheffield.

Tommy's other love in life, apart from Wednesday, drinking and the odd woman, was music. The talk was about this new youth explosion 'Punk Rock' and especially the Sex Pistols. They were due to play the City Hall on the 17th of December, but it was cancelled. "Well I think it's a load of crap" said most of the group. But Tommy thought it would catch on once they were allowed to play. "It will be dead within 12 months" said Shess. But Tommy was not being drawn on the subject.

It was now 1977 and, after the heat wave of the summer, it was now colder in Britain than in Iceland. This took a heavy toll on all the sporting fixtures that should have been taking place. January the 8th saw Wednesday and United both at home. The Owls were playing Brighton and the Blades had the mouth-watering visit of Newcastle United in the F.A. Cup. After the boys had witnessed a dull 0-0 draw with the Seagulls, they headed into town. They had planned to meet in the Claymore after the game.

The city was full to bursting with the boys from the Northeast. Once inside the place was still full of Geordies and it was difficult to get served. The boys positioned themselves near the stairs that led down to the toilets. This is where they always stood when they had arranged to meet some mates who had not been to the game. The plan was to have a few drinks around town and finish up in the Daisy. The rest of the party arrived late as usual and the boys moved on, leaving the pub to the mercy of the brown ale brigade.

Most of the Newcastle fans had left the town after creating havoc all afternoon, but still the lads bumped into odd pockets of black and white clad supporters. Tommy bumped into three mates who had been to the Lane. "How's it been today lads?" he asked. "Trouble with a capital T" was the reply. "There's been fighting everywhere in the pubs, on London Road, in the ground, you name it. Them Geordie bastards have caused it." The three joined Tommy and the lads and headed for the Golden Ball. On entering the pub it seemed to be quieter than normal. There didn't seem to be many in, the reason being it was still early and the other side of the bar had a group of Geordies in. The two rooms were not really separated as such and there was only one toilet, which was situated near the back of the building.

The boys had been served and were stood chatting when Shess asked Tommy to hold his beer while he went for a piss. On entering the piss hole a pissed up Geordie spilt beer all down Shess. Now even though he wasn't too chuffed about it he remembered how many times he been in that state. But what really annoyed him was the fact he showed no manners and didn't even apologise. Forgetting all about wanting a piss he pursued the Geordie git into the other side. "Excuse me mate but don't they teach you manners in Newcastle?" pointing to his soaking jacket. "Thas just spilt all the beer down me and just fucked off" replied Shess. The Geordie just turned to his mates and laughed. This really pissed Shess off so he just belted the bastard sending him flying. The Geordies just went for him, sending him back in the direction he had come from. The rest of the lads were oblivious to this until they saw him battling with the black and white hordes. The boys now joined in and the pub was really emptying with the fans giving it all they'd got.

Out on the street the Geordies were really up against it. Not only did they have the boys to deal with, but even passing women were giving it to them with their brollies. The Geordies were now legging it away from the Ball in the direction of High Street. The fun was over for the time being, so they went back inside the pub. Shess was still fuming about his brand new leather jacket that cost him a packet from Tramps on King Street. "Give it a rest" laughed Billy. "You could have got a good one for all that money!" he added.

Tommy and the lads finished the evening off in the Daisy. Tommy liked it in there as not only did they play good music but his Auntie worked behind the bar, so sometimes when it was busy she would serve Tom and then move on to the next customer, leaving Tom with a round of free drinks. The rest of the weekend passed off without incident.

The next week saw the country hit by blizzards and people struggled to get about their daily routines. This lasted about a week and, in the meantime, the Owls were going great guns. By the 15th of January the Owls had accumulated 29 points with victory at Northampton. The next game was away to Walsall. The boys had decided on the Soccer Special being run by British Rail. The fare was two quid and it arrived in Walsall at 2pm. The weather was not very good on them arriving at the ground, so they decided to go on the covered section on the side terrace. Most of the Owls fans were crammed into this section, but some had got into the home section and were causing the usual mayhem. The game was a disaster in more ways than one. Wednesday got thrashed 5-1 and a barrier collapsed injuring one or two fans. The coppers were a bit heavy handed and one or two of the coppers helmets were flying about. All in all the day was a right wash out and Tommy could not wait to get home.

The rest of January and February saw the Owls bring their grand total of points to 35, which was 11 points better off than the same time last season. The 26th of February saw the Owls return to Chesterfield. The boys decided on the train but realised there would be a larger police presence than last season to contain any outbreaks of violence.

On arriving in Chesterfield the boys made their way towards the ground and found one or two pubs in the Newbold area of the town. Ray now fully recovered from his frightening experience down at Millwall wanted to know what the plans were. "We will split into small groups and get onto their end" said Bob. "I can see there'll be quite a few of our lot on their Kop" added Tommy. The lads made their way to the ground from the opposite end from were the majority of the Owls fans would be coming. Tommy thought that the major concentration of police would be patrolling the route from the Station to the ground, and not have too many out in the suburbs.

Tommy bought his usual programme and headed into the Chesterfield end. Once inside he took up his position to the left-hand side of the goal and buried his head in his programme. The ground was now quickly filling up ,and the opposite end of the ground was full of Wednesdayites. Tommy was scanning the terraces for friendly faces, but could not see too many so he decided to make his way to a different position. Then he saw a small group of Owls fans in the bottom corner of the Kop. Tommy thought that this was a bad position to be in, penned in that bottom corner. Suddenly up went the chant "East Bank Republican Army." The lads were goading the Spireites to come and get them. Across they charged from the safety of the middle of the Kop. The Owls numbers suddenly multiplied and what started as a small group turned into a large mob. On seeing this, some supporters tried to come across the pitch like last season, but this time the police were ready. The coppers poured in to keep the rival factions apart and the anorak and scarf brigade made for the safety of the pitch. The police pushed the Chesterfield supporters back towards the middle and contained the Owls fans down the left-hand side, opening up a gap between the rivals. With the game in progress it seemed better to contain the fans in this position than try and remove them to the Wednesday section, or eject them from the ground. What was the point in throwing out a couple of hundred football fans to wonder round the streets unsupervised? Insults were exchanged across no mans land, and the odd supporter was getting ejected, but on the whole it wasn't too bad.

Then something happened to change all that. Chesterfield scored and they surged towards the Wednesdayites. The coppers momentarily lost control and it was time to party. Fists and Boots were flying everywhere. Fans were getting thrown down the terracing and Tommy and the lads were landing some beauties onto the bodies of the country bumpkins. It all lasted no more than five minutes but seemed to go on for ages.

The coppers regained control and in came reinforcements. The police seemed to outnumber the Owls fans 2 to 1, and the rest of the game really passed off without further incident.

The game ended in defeat for the Owls 2-0, but now was the task of getting to the station in one piece. The boys knew that the Chesterfield mob would be gunning for them, and their numbers seemed to be dwindling. "If we stick together we should be O.K." said Shess. The coppers had soon disappeared and left the boys to fend for themselves and, as they walked towards the station, the Chesterfield mob were grouped near the Town Hall. "Lets go for it" shouted Ray, and with that what remained of their group charged at them screaming. Football supporters were scattering everywhere as the rivals slugged it out in the middle of the road. Heavily outnumbered the lads were doing their best to keep from being hammered. A large number of Wednesday fans, that were heading for the station, heard the commotion and charged up the street. It was now a full-scale battle that only ended with the arrival of scores of coppers. It was time now to avoid being nicked as the police were grabbing at anyone they could lay their hands on. This was the last place any Sheffielder wanted to end up in court after what happened last year.

Most of the boys were accounted for except for Mick and Terry. They had not been seen since leaving the ground. It turned out that both had been locked up for threatening behaviour and in the subsequent court case were both fined £110. Wednesday, by the end of March were still picking up points and had a chance of promotion. Then came their best sequence of results since taking eleven points from six games back in November/December. After drawing with Shrewsbury, the Owls beat Grimsby, York City, Rotherham and Preston.

Now for the away trip to Crystal Palace. This had been booked for ages. A guy called Vinnie ran the bus and it was stopping in London until midnight. On the Friday night the lads had arranged to meet in the Claymore and have a few drinks around town as Manchester United were playing Leeds at Hillsborough in the Semi Final of the F.A. Cup on that Saturday. Whilst sitting in the Claymore having a drink, these five lads walked in. Tommy knew them from the Daisy, which had started having a Punk night once a week. Tommy also knew they were Wednesdayites that were going to Palace on Vinnie's coach. The five lads got their drinks and joined Tommy and his mates. "This is Bob, Billy, Chas, Gaz and Mick" said Tom. The one Tommy knew the best was a lad named Macca who, like Tom, was really into Punk. Macca introduced his mates. "This is Drum. He's into Punk and the others are Willie, Brent and Kevin who are Soul boys" added Macca. The new found mates moved out into the night air and wandered around town, calling in at their usual watering holes. Macca told the lads that they were going to the all-nighter at Samantha's, and asked if they fancied coming. Chas, Mick and Gaz were not all that keen, but Tommy and Bob were up for it. Billy said that he would see them in Pond Street in the morning and off he went.

The lads made the Howard Hotel their last port of call, before moving onto Sammy's. Once inside there was a group of Man U Fans hogging the bar. As the boys squeezed past to get served Brent said to this Red "Shift you fat twat. We can't get served." Tommy thought this one doesn't mess about and comes straight to the point. Because the fat one was taken aback by Brent's remarks he said "I'll show you who's a fat twat, Get outside." Brent was out of the door like a shot, but on everybody leaving the pub there was no sign of Brent. "He's bottled it" said the fat one. Just then Brent came hurtling round the corner brandishing a rubbish bin which he calmly planted into the fat one's face. The blob fell like a ton of bricks, with blood everywhere. Brent was victorious and the Reds pissed off.

Back inside the pub Tommy was well impressed with his new found friends. They supped up and moved on to Sammy's. It was not really Tommy's cup of tea, with the lads parading round in their long leather coats, but the music was all right. The night seemed to fly by and, when they emerged into the morning air, Tommy felt like shit. The party moved onto Pond Street to get some brekkie.

The coach was due to leave for London at 9am. As the lads were waiting outside the Threpenny Bit kiosk, a right mob of Manchester supporters were heading their way. Tommy didn't feel they were a threat to the boys because they only numbered seven. But then nightmare of all nightmares: who's at the front? The fat git who Brent had clobbered. The fat one shouted "That's the bastard who did this." The lads shot off in all directions. Tommy and Willie shot down by the side of the Penny Black in the direction of the steps that led up into Fitzallan Square, with most of the mob in pursuit. On reaching the steps the mob had caught up with the two. Willie turned to face the mob and from inside his sheepskin pulled out a razor. This stopped the Reds in their tracks and Tommy stood at Wills side. "I know were going to get a good kicking but who wants some of this?" he asked the mob. Nobody in their right mind is going to tackle somebody with one of those in their hands. As the pair backed up the stairs the Reds had decided that they wanted to see the semi in one piece, and anyway they probably didn't know the fat twat anyway.

Tommy and Willie walked back towards Pond Street. "Do you always carry that?" Tommy asked Willie. "No, only when I think there could be trouble" he replied. The bus arrived and the lads were quickly on board, settling into their seats. The bus was quite full by the time Vinnie came round.

58

"It's £2.50 and that includes the tip for the driver" he said. "Where's the coach dropping us off?" asked Tommy "The coach is dropping at Waterloo Station so we can get a train to the match" added Vinnie. Tommy thought to himself that they were cutting it fine, to be at the game for kick off. Vinnie told the lads that the bus would be leaving bang on midnight from the Victoria Coach Station. The driver made good time down to London. Vinnie's coaches never stopped for a toilet break so there was always a bucket at the front of the bus. Tommy liked travelling with Vinnie's boys, because he knew that all the bus would stick together, and that Vinnie didn't allow any anorak and scarfers on his bus.

Thornton Heath Station was the destination for this motley crew of football supporters, thus allowing the lads to stroll through the High Street on their way to the ground. It had turned 2.30 when they finally alighted at the station, so the chances of meeting any opposition were very slim. Once inside the ground the lads joined the rest of the travelling Owls fans massed on the side terrace. The Palace fans were also on the side terrace, but nothing major happened, just the odd missile, but it was mostly insults that were traded.

The Owls had a disastrous day going down 4-0 and suffering there heaviest defeat since the 5-1 mauling by Walsall. Once outside the ground fighting broke out between the rival supporters. The police were finding it difficult to keep the factions apart. Vinnie's lot were in the thick of things and so was Tommy, the lads and his newfound friends. The Wednesday ran the Palace ragged, leaving them spread all over the place. The police had now restored order and were ushering the fans onto the coaches for the return home. "Come on lads, get on your bus" this copper said. Vinnie told the officer that the bus was somewhere in the middle of London, with the driver probably fast asleep. What was the plod going to do with this lot? Tommy thought. The police decided to escort them to the station, but Tommy thought this a bad idea. The boys would be a right target for the Palace fans that would be making their way to the same station. But, then again, the boys would all stick together.

Marching down Thornton High Street the lads swaggered like a conquering army that had just liberated the said town. Once at the Station the police held the boys back until all the home supporters had boarded the train. When the next train came along the boys jumped on board and settled down for the trip back to Waterloo. The police had left the boys to fend for themselves.

As the train approached Norbury the windows started to shatter around them. The Palace fans had jumped off and lay in wait for the next train. When the train stopped some of the boys jumped off, but the attackers were long gone. Luckily no-one was injured but they'd had a lucky escape. When they finally got back to Waterloo, Tommy and the boys decided to stay round Lambeth and sample some of the traditional cockney hospitality. The boys had done their battling for one day and now was the time to have a few beers and enjoy what London had to offer. The first pub they went in was a quiet little pub, with a jukebox and a pool table but little else. Tommy loved to play pool but was not very good. They spent most of the evening in this pub just chilling out. The new lads seemed to get on well with Tommy's mates, and Tommy asked them if they fancied Tranmere for the last away game of the season, to be played on Friday night. "Webbo's taking the van but we can fit you in if you want" Tommy said. Macca told Tommy that the lads would definitely go. The lads moved on and finished the evening off around Victoria.

Once back on the coach and heading for home, Tommy commented that Vinnie knew how to organise a day out, and next season they would travel with him more regularly.

After the defeat at Palace Wednesday were destined for another season in the third, after beating Peterborough at Hillsborough. The Owls lost at Brighton leaving only two games to go; the Friday fixture at Tranmere and finally at home to Oxford. Tommy finished off the weekend in his usual haunts and was up bright an early Monday and off to work he went. Chris the apprentice asked Tommy if he could go with the lads to Tranmere. Tom told him that he thought it would be all right but would let him know later on in the week. The week dragged by because Tommy was once again skint and needed all his money for this weekend, knowing that with the game being on Friday the boys would be out all day Saturday.

Friday eventually arrived and Tommy and Chris finished at dinner so they went into town to meet Macca and his mates. Once off the bus they headed for the Claymore where the lads were meeting. Inside Tommy approached the boys who were standing by the doorway. He reached across and tried to remove the morning's newspaper from Willies pocket. As Tommy grabbed at it Willie pushed his hand away telling him to leave it where it was. "What's up with him?" Tommy asked Macca. Macca told Tommy that the paper was not for reading but it was Willies new invention. "Willie, let Tommy have a feel at your paper" said Macca. Tommy lifted the paper out of Willie's pocket. "Bloody hell what's in here?" shouted Tommy. Willie told him it was a fitter's spanner that was carefully wrapped inside the Daily Mirror. Willie was going to try it out tonight at Tranmere if there was any trouble. Tommy told the lads that the Transit was leaving the Royal at four, so they had a couple in town then headed up there.

The lads arrived at the pub just before three and the landlord let them stay until Webbo picked them up. It was quite a good turnout and Webbo was counting the numbers in his head. "There's sixteen Tommy. How we going to all fit in?" said Webbo. "With difficulty" replied Bob. The journey to Merseyside was a nightmare and Tommy was now realising that the Transit was coming to the end of its days. Finally the lads reached their destination and crawled out of what seemed like the black hole of Calcutta! Webbo parked the bus away from the ground and descended on to the local watering hole. The lads walked through the door to be greeted by the landlord. Tommy said "Aare we alright for a drink mate"? To this the landlord replied "No problem" in a broad scouse accent. The boys indulged in two of their favourite pastimes; drinking and talking football. Macca and Tommy were playing pool, and Macca was easily beating Tommy. No matter how many times Tommy played this game he never got any better.

The time now was getting on so the boys made their way towards the ground. On leaving the pub the boys thanked the landlord for his hospitality. On reaching the ground Billy commented that the crowd around the ground was poor. "I don't think there's many here tonight" he said. On entering the ground the turn out from both sides was poor. "There can only be a couple of thousand here tonight" said Shess. "Well what do you expect? It's a Friday night and everybody's out on the fucking piss!" said Tommy.

The game passed off without incident and the Owls lost 1-0. On leaving the ground all hell broke loose. "Where's all these bastards come from?" shouted Macca. "Well they've certainly not been to the game" added Billy. There must have been a mob of over 100 youths confronting the Owls fans as they left the ground. "They've got to be Everton or Liverpool" said Willie. The Wednesday fans tried to organise themselves the best they could but, on looking around, Tommy realised that the majority of Owls fans present were the anorak and scarf brigade. The boys seemed to be totally outnumbered but they had no option but to stand and fight. Willie was going at it with great gusto with his new-found friend, and dispatching the Scousers left right and centre. The lads battled with the Scousers and were getting the upper hand. Other Wednesdayites, who very rarely got involved, were joining the hostilities, probably because the aggressors had not even been to the match and had just been waiting for the match to end to attack the Wednesday supporters. The fighting seemed to last forever, but usually it was only ten minutes tops before the coppers moved in.

With the fighting over it was back to the black hole of Calcutta that was Webbo's van for the trip back over the Pennines. On the journey home Tommy was amazed at the way the new-found tool had stood up to the rigours of battle and he must have one for the following season.

Tommy was reflecting on the highs and lows of the nearly ended season that was 1976-77. The high points were the victories over Grimsby and Wolves in the cup. Also many victories in the league that outnumbered the defeats for a change, the fighting at Port Vale, Chesterfield and Lincoln and the encounters with Newcastle and Manchester United in Sheffield. The low points were the experience that they encountered at Millwall and the defeats at Walsall and Crystal Palace and also Preston. So on the whole 1976-77 had not been too bad a season. The Owls finished it off with a victory over Oxford at Hillsborough and finished in a respectable eighth position. Tommy thought that next season was going to be extra special, especially with the new additions to the group.

All the smiling faces walking down Penistone Road to see Jack Charlton's Aces 1977 - 1978

The summer of 1977 saw the Queen's Silver Jubilee and the explosion of Punk Rock onto the British youth. Tommy was really into it and had been to see quite a few bands such as The Ramones, The Jam and The Stranglers to name but a few. This put an added strain on Tommy's slim resources. "I don't know what I'm going to do once the football season starts" he told Billy. "You'll either have to find a better paid job or choose between Punk and Football" Billy added. This was not a dilemma that Tom had to face just yet because the season did not kick off until the 13th of August. Wednesday were at home to Doncaster Rovers in the first round of the League Cup to kick off the new season. But the night before the lads went to the Top Rank to see The Boomtown Rats, a Punk band from Ireland. Tommy had been looking forward to this for a long time and had even dragged Billy along even though he didn't like the music.

The group had only been on stage a few moments when some bastard in the crowd threw a bottle, which hit the lead singer cutting his head. This brought the evening's entertainment to a close. Macca was furious commenting that it was the Disco types that had caused the problem. They had just come in to cause trouble and if it was trouble they wanted then they had come to the right place. As the boys approached a group of lads at the bar. The bastards found what had happened rather amusing. Willie asked the tossers what they were laughing at to which one replied "Not very hard these punks are they." To this Willie nutted him and the lads set about doing what they do best, that is giving grief to those who deserve it. The contest was too one sided to the lads liking because the disco boys were not a match for 20 battle hardened football hooligans who just steamed through them like a knife through butter.

With Friday's jollies to an end the boys went their separate ways and arranged to meet in the Claymore before the match the next day. The lads didn't expect too much activity at Hillsborough but the game was a great start for the Owls, winning 5-2. The return was at Belle Vue on Tuesday night and the boys met in town for the short train journey to Doncaster. The boys got to the ground and went on the side terrace that housed most of the Donny fans. It wasn't long before trouble erupted and it sent the anorak and scarf brigade scurrying for the safety of the pitch and leaving the terrace to the ones who needed it most, the like minded soccer thugs that the British Media called a threat to the lovely game.

Then disaster struck in the fighting that followed. Tommy was really going for it, and enjoying every minute, when this chap grabbed him and sent him tumbling down the terrace coming to rest against the perimeter wall. The man knelt across Tommy and pulled out his warrant card saying the immortal words "Your nicked!" The plain clothed copper had Tommy bangs to right and led him to the holding cell where he was to spend the rest of the evening and having coffee spilt all down him by the country's finest upholders of the law.

After the game, which the Owls won 3-0, Tommy was charged with threatening behaviour and bailed to appear at

Doncaster Magistrate's Court at a later date. Sitting in his cell Tommy was thinking what fun the others would be having in his absence. Finally he was let out into the night air just after the last train had gone back to Sheffield. With hardly any money on him and wondering what to do, another Wednesday fan was also let out of the nick. Tommy asked the lad if he would share a cab back to Sheffield, to which the lad replied "I live in Wath" which is nearer to Doncaster than Sheffield. But the lad told Tommy that he would not see him stranded and that he could share his cab. Tommy thought this rather charitable because the lad was going well out of his way.

Tommy was dropped off at the bottom of Prince of Wales Road and the cab disappeared back onto the Parkway. Tommy still had a long walk home and was totally bollocksed when he put his key in the door. Tommy thought it best not to worry the family about his forthcoming court case and decided to keep it to himself for the time being.

Wednesday started off the league campaign with two draws at home to Swindon and Walsall. Then came the Cup game at Blackpool, which was on a Tuesday night. Nobody was working that day but, if they were, they just didn't turn in. Tommy had organised with Webbo to take the Transit. "How many are going?" he asked. Tommy said "I just told them to be at the Royal for nine o'clock." When Webbo arrived with the van he also had mad Frank with him. He told Tommy that they needed to call and have the exhaust welded before they could set off.

Tommy did a quick head count and thought how the hell are they going to fit 20 in Webbo's Tranny? It was a right squeeze getting everyone in but it was only just over two hours to Blackpool, although it would be nearer to three in the Transit. Eventually the weary travellers emerged from inside the van coughing and spluttering after spending the last three hours breathing in Webbo's finest exhaust fumes. "Let's get some nice sea air in the lungs before we choke to death" said Macca. "Not used to our executive travel quite yet Macca?" laughed Chas.

The lads spent the day just wondering around having the odd drink but mostly just chilling out around the pleasure beach. Webbo told the lads that after the match if anybody got separated that they would meet in the Castle pub near the Tower. The boys spent the last couple of hours before the game in the Castle before moving on to the match.

The Wednesday fans were situated on the large terrace behind the goal and had brought a large following. The game passed off with not much happening on the terracing but, on the field, Wednesday played well and the game finished 2-2.

Outside the ground most of the supporters were just getting on the coaches for the journey home, but the lads grouped together to walk back into town to meet at the Castle. The Wednesday fans taking this route numbered no more than a hundred. Then the inevitable happened. The Blackpool fans came at them from the direction of the town. The lads grouped together and went at it with the usual vigour, sending the Seasiders on their way. Some tried to climb the fencing that ran the length of the thoroughfare to escape the fighting but were dragged back and given a good seeing to.

With Blackpool firmly dealt with the boys were on a high. "I can't believe it would be that easy" said Willie as the boys moved on to the Castle. Webbo told them to be at the van for 10.15 so they just had time for one more pint and then they would be on their way. Just then Ray came in and told the lads that there was a tasty bunch waiting outside the pub and they had probably seen the boys enter the Castle and were waiting for them to come out. Webbo had parked the van on Newton Drive, which was a fair walk from the Castle, up Albert Road.

Macca told the lads that if Blackpool wanted them then it was their turn to make the first move. The group moved out of the pub and headed up Albert Road with the Seasiders tagging along. It was starting to get boring, Willie was growing impatient and Macca was having a problem holding him back. Then as the lads moved into Church Street the Seasiders came from everywhere, and the boys stood their ground. Like a flash Willie pulled out his trusty companion and went for it like a man possessed, having the enemy quickly on their toes. Macca was none too pleased with him. "We could have done them without that" he shouted at him. Willie walked off like a naughty schoolboy that had been told off by the Headmaster. At the van Webbo wanted to know why they were so late to which Tommy told him that they had encountered some hostile locals.

The journey home was a nightmare. Not only did we have the exhaust fumes and cigarette smoke, but also all the bodily functions that occur when the boys have been on the beer all day. Finally, the motley crew arrived home just after two and went their separate ways. It was back to work tomorrow for Tommy, and Chris the apprentice would be going none stop about what a great time they'd had in Blackpool. Tommy didn't need all this hassle at work and would be telling Chris to button it because he didn't want the management knowing what he got up to in his spare time.

On arriving at work Tommy was told to go and see the manager straight away. All sorts of things were going through Tommy's mind to why Mr. Marshall wanted to see him. Tommy knocked on the door and was told to come in. "I'll not keep you long, but what it is, Charlie the fork truck driver is leaving at the end of the month and I wondered if you would like his job. You would have to take a test but if you were successful it would mean more hours and more money" he told

Tommy. Tommy was delighted with the news and rushed back to tell Chris. The only draw back with the new job was that Tommy would have to work Saturday mornings to load the lorries so they could set off first thing Monday mornings.

Tommy was not due to start the new job until the end of September, so it gave him plenty of time to organise himself. Saturday saw the Owls lose at Bury 3-0 and then were defeated by Shrewsbury 1-0 and Chester 2-1. Saturday the 17th of September saw the Owls at Port Vale and Webbo was again taking the van. Also, this time, the party included a couple of kids so it was decided that the lads would give the home section a miss this season. But on arriving at the ground the queues for the Wednesday end were horrendous, so the party decided on the home section after all. Not anticipating any trouble the group settled near the front to the left hand side of the goal, with the kids stood against the perimeter wall.

Just before kick off Billy noticed a small group, numbering no more than twenty, making their way towards the boys, with this extra large skinhead at the fore. "I can't believe they're coming for us" said Billy, "Get the kids over the wall" he shouted as the hostile group ran at them. Billy, Tommy and Willie with the help of Ray, Brent and Bob were doing the best they could until their party had got on to the perimeter track. Then they had to make a hasty retreat. Once on the track side Willie was goading the skinhead to follow, and Mad Frank was going banana's at this copper, telling him he was forty years old married with two kids and to look what them bastards have done to his jeans. With his jean leg in tatters Frank was going mental as the group dropped into the side terrace.

They spent the remainder of the game watching the Owls fight out a goalless draw. On making their way out of the ground and back round to where the Transit was parked, who should be coming in the opposite direction, but the big

70

skinhead who had caused all the bollocks before the game. Jokingly Ray said "That's the bastard who ripped thi' jeans Frank". To this Frank flew at the startled skin sending him flying and giving him a good leathering. Everybody just stopped in their tracks and watched Frank tear him to pieces. Fortunately, for the skinhead, the coppers jumped in to spoil Franks fun and dragged him off the battered Skin. Frank told the Police that he had taken his kids on the home end and was attacked by that bastard and his mates, and they had ripped his jeans. The Police told Frank that he was a known troublemaker and they would not be arresting Frank for assaulting him. Frank told the startled copper "Give me ten more minutes with him and he'll not cause you any more trouble!" Even though Franks offer seemed tempting the Policeman just laughed and walked away.

Once back inside the Tranny Frank still wanted to finish off the skinhead and told Webbo to follow the gang of Vale fans. The Transit finished up in Burslem bus station parked behind the bus that the skin had got on. The lads were now trying to calm Frank down and stopping him doing something stupid and getting himself nicked. So Tommy suggested that they head back to the ground and find some other fans to do battle with.

On driving past the ground and passing numerous anorak and scarfers they stumbled on what looked like a bunch of like-minded souls. Tommy told Webbo to pull into the garage forecourt and let the lads out but keep Frank in the van, because he would do some serious damage the mood he was in. The lads positioned themselves ready to do battle with the oncoming mob and as they grew close the lads went at it sending the Vale retreating. Fists and Boots were flying everywhere and the lads were well on top. Then two Chinese kids came running at the boys like something out of a Bruce

Lee film. One kicked Tommy, sending him flying against a shop window, which luckily didn't break. Vale started back up the hill throwing milk bottles at the Wednesday boys, not only did they have the bottles to contend with, but the two Chinese were not helping matters. Just then Ray and Brent went at the Chinese with a couple of ratchets they'd grabbed from the van sending them retreating back into their shop.

It was now raining bottles and the poor woman at the traffic lights was getting her lovely car pounded with the Co-op's finest. The jollities were nearly over as the boys ran to the van and they jumped in, gesturing to the pursuing pack that they were all tossers. This time it was Baslow before the happy souls stopped for a drink. Frank was still on about his trousers, the ratchet boys were on about their encounter with the Chinese, Tommy was nursing a small lump on his head and they all commented on how the Skinhead would never forget Frank.

By the end of September, Tommy had started his new job and enjoyed the added responsibility of being left to get on with loading the lorries. He had got permission to load up the trucks on a Friday when the Owls were playing away, and the management didn't mind because the job was getting done.

The Owls were having a disastrous start to the season and Len Ashurst was under increasing pressure to turn it around. The Blades had all ready parted company with their boss Jimmy Sirrell, but that did not interest the boys one bit. By the end of September the Owls had only got 4 points from the first 8 games, but this didn't bother Tommy as he had more pressing business to hand. It was Friday night and he had five lorries to load before he could go home and get himself ready, because it was Portsmouth tomorrow and Vinnie was running a bus from the Daisy.

Tommy got home from work at 8.30 that evening. His mum was so proud of him taking added responsibility at work. He had a quick bite to eat jumped into the bath and was out of the house by 9.30. He met the rest of the boys in the Royal. Waiting for him was Billy, Bob, Chas, Archie and Shess. The others they were meeting down town in the Claymore, they just managed a quick one then it was into the Daisy. On entering the Club they were met by Vinnie who told the boys he'd booked them twelve seats on the bus, "That's right, us six plus Willie, Macca, Brent, Trevor, Ray and Drum". The boys settled down to sink a few beers but, unfortunately for Tommy, his Auntie wasn't working so he would have to pay for his. At 2.30 the boys left the club and boarded the coach. Tommy looked around and nodded to most of the lads who went to Palace. "There's a good turn out for the trip South" he informed the boys, and they should be there for breakfast. The lads settled down to get some kip, especially Tom, who had been working all day loading up his lorries.

The journey South was a tedious one and, with the distance just over 200 miles, it was going to take a few hours. Vinnie did not want the boys getting there too early so they stopped quite frequently. At one stop just outside Oxford they encountered a coach full of Manchester United supporters on their way to Old Trafford. They were from Winchester but were the everyday run of the mill football supporters that posed no threat to a coach load of footballs finest. That did not stop the boys rifling their coach and returning with hands laden with their ill-gotten gains. The complete haul consisted of Manchester's finest hats and scarves, not to mention the cans of ale.

The boys went on their merry way and were down the A34 towards Newbury when they got a pull from the Constabulary. As quick as a flash the hats and scarves were put through the skylight and left on the roof. As for the ale, that had been quickly consumed. The officer boarded the bus and told the boys he had received a complaint from some supporters that a coach carrying Sheffield Wednesday supporters had boarded their coach and had stole numerous items. As the copper examined the coach and found nothing so the lads were quickly back on their way, unfortunately they were not too quick at retrieving the goodies from the roof and one or two fell by the roadside.

They arrived at their destination at around 7.30am and were quickly left to their own devices by the coach driver. The party wandered around trying to find a café so they could get something to eat. In the meantime, Macca stumbled on a works van that had conveniently left them a football in the back. This soon turned into a full-scale game of football from one end of the High Street to the other. The ball was being booted everywhere, even people on their way to work were joining in, and not a copper in sight. The ball suddenly fell at Ray's feet and, with an all mighty swing of his right leg, sent the ball sailing over the rooftops never to be seen again. Vinnie suggested that they all split into smaller groups and meet up again at the bus station later. This seemed a good idea because it wouldn't be too long before the police would be on their case. Tommy's twelve headed for a café near the train station and settled down to have a bite to eat.

It was now 9.30 and most of the boys were at the bus station. When they had all gathered together they descended on Southsea to check out the seaside town. It wasn't long before one or two were on the rob, flitting from one shop to another seeing what they could pick up. It was arranged that the boys would meet at the big boozer situated near the amusements. Not everyone had made the rendezvous point when a group of denim clad bovver boys with blue and white scarves tightly pulled around their necks stood outside the boozer. Not a word was spoken by the Sheffield Boys. Not wanting to give the game away just yet they just stood there silent. Then the Dick Emery look-a-like opened his gob, "Should have some fun with them Northern bastards this afternoon boys" he smirked. That was the last time they saw him with a smile on his face as Chas belted him with his favourite spanner wrapped in the newspaper. The Pompey boys didn't know what hit them as the boys were going mental. Vinnie was well pissed off that he had missed it all.

As the jubilant Wednesdayites went to get the bus back to Pompey, the police were heading in the other direction. With all the lads on the bus and heading away from Southsea, the bus was suddenly stopped by a load of coppers. The police boarded the bus and allowed the ordinary passengers to get off the bus, just leaving Vinnie's party onboard. Three coppers came up the stairs and told the boys that they had reports of a group of lads fitting their description who had been involved in an assault, and that numerous shops had items stolen. They were now being taken straight to the police station for questioning. The bus dropped them off at the station and they were all marched in like soldiers on parade. Left on board the bus was an array of discarded newspapers that the plod failed to notice, to everyone's delight. They now had the prove that it was the boys who had caused all these problems and not some other like-minded souls and, as no one in their right mind is going to own up to it, Tommy didn't fancy their job. They marched the boys in about ten at a time so that the shopkeepers could have a good look and, as a result, five of the group were charged on suspicion of theft. Now came the serious one, assault on the Dick Emery look-a-like. As the lads walked in they could hardly control themselves with him now wearing a turban. But they took their hat off to the man, or was it turban, as he didn't finger anybody for the alleged assault. It was now 2pm and they started to let the boys out in groups of threes and fours to split them all up, sending them out of different exits. That was a complete waste of time as the boys had all ready arranged to meet in the boozer they'd spotted on entering the nick. Once the boys had all gathered in the pub they got their party together and headed for the match.

On approaching the stadium Brent wanted to visit the home, section but the boys were being monitored by the local police. Anyway Macca told him that Pompey would be coming for them. The boys made their way round to the visitors section and positioned themselves to the right hand side of the goal near to the back. The side section to their right contained quite a few of Portsmouth's finest, and only a small gate separated the boys from them. There had been small outbreaks of violence in and around the ground, but as the lads had spent most of the day in the nick they'd missed it.

Wednesday needed to start picking up points and had started brightly against Portsmouth and were doing O.K when the whistle went for half-time. The boys quickly moved to the refreshment bar and were soon in the queue ordering something nice and hot. As the boys stood about chatting the Pompey Boys made their move and converged onto them. Before they could raise a fist in anger, tea and Bovril were flying in their direction. The lads were at it with some of the South's finest and they were enjoying every minute, especially Brent who was connecting like a prize fighter on a mission. Chas was confronted by a weird looking guy who'd removed his shoes and just stood there Kung Fu style. Chas gave him such a crack he was soon being dispatched down the terrace with the help of an array of the best fashionable footwear money can buy. The police were quickly in to restore some kind of order and fun was finally over.

Wednesday fought out a credible 2-2 draw to take their total for the season to 5 points. Outside the ground the coaches were all lined up to take the fans home, and the police were having a job on keeping the rivals apart. Vinnie's party was in full swing and you'd got to hand it to Vinnie, he really had got a proper little army together. The Pompey Bovver Boys could not handle their determined and organised advances. They just attacked like a swarm of bees.

The coaches were now mostly on their way and their numbers were dwindling fast. The police wanted to know where the coach was. Vinnie informed the top brass that they were staying on for a drink and returning home later. The officer in charge told his men to locate their coach and get it here pronto. Thirty minutes later the coach arrived and the driver was told, in no uncertain terms, that his party was leaving now and he was not to stop for any reason. The lads reluctantly boarded the bus and set off. The bus had only gone about half a mile when the driver stopped at a set of traffic lights. Off the lads jumped and straight into a boozer. In the mayhem that followed things were getting lifted and the coppers were running out of patience with the boys and getting really pissed off. Eventually they'd had their fun for the day and left the coppers in peace, once again heading back to Gods own county which was Yorkshire.

The return was a nightmare at every junction of every Motorway. The coppers of all the different forces were keeping a careful watch on the coach. Tommy had a word with Vinnie about getting organised for the visit to Bradford, "If we don't go together it would be such a waste after witnessing our party in action together" he told Vinnie. Wednesday had so many little pockets of hooligans that it was very rare for them to get organised and band together. If only they could turn this fifty into say two hundred like-minded souls, they'd be a match for anyone.

Tommy spent the rest of the weekend just chilling out after what was so far the best trip of the season. Tuesday night saw the Owls visit Preston and once again all the different factions went their separate ways. Tommy and the boys were once again at the mercy of the Transit. The Tranny was not as full as the Blackpool trip, but it was still a good turn out. Webbo parked the van well away from the ground and it was quite a walk through the park to the ground. It wasn't a bad night weather wise for a night game in October, and the lads so far had not encountered any North Enders. Half way into the park the boys came across a large group numbering no more than thirty, but how many of that group were up for it? Macca said "Lets see what there made of," and with that the boys went for it. It was quite clear from the off that these were your normal everyday supporters, and not into violence, so the confrontation ended sooner than it had started. The boys took no joy out of attacking football fans that were just there for the football. As the Preston fans legged it towards the ground the boys settled back down and leisurely strolled to the match. On leaving the park the boys noticed some people pointing them out to the police. "Quick," said Tommy "The coppers are coming our way." The lads made for the safety of the crowd and didn't want the thought of being nicked to spoil an evening's entertainment.

Once inside the stadium the boys settled back and watched the Owls once again put in a lacklustre performance going down 2-1. Just before the final whistle the boys met up with Vinnie's lot and moved out of the ground and around to the home section. It was decided that they would attempt to confront Preston on them leaving the ground. As Tommy looked around he could see that there was a good selection of boys that would stand their ground no matter what. Preston were still celebrating their victory when the lads entered the home end. Many people were making their way out of the Kop, but they were not the target. The boys had only just got up the steps when they came for them, but they stood their ground like Tommy knew they would, and fighting erupted between the rival gangs, spilling out onto the huge car park that fronted the stadium. Fans were fighting between the cars and coaches and Wednesday fans spilling out of the visitors end quickly joined in, and sent the North Enders on their way home with their tails between their legs. The boys quickly grouped back together and made for the darkness of the park, to get out of the way of the local constabulary.

Once back to the safety of the van the talk quickly turned to the disastrous start to the season. "We can't go on like this or we'll be in the fourth division" said Billy, commenting that we'd only accumulated five points so far. The manager, Len Ashurst, was under extreme pressure to turn it around, after the Owls had finished a credible eighth the season before. The following day, as Tommy headed home from work, the local paper ran the headline that Wednesday sacked Ashurst. "That's all we need right now" he thought to himself. Wednesday put Ken Knighton in temporary charge for the visit of Chesterfield.

At work and in the pub Tommy and his mates were wondering what lay ahead for managerless Wednesday. On the day of the game against Chesterfield, the boys met as usual in the Claymore, and talk was not about having a confrontation with the Spireites, but on the precarious situation that the Owls found themselves in. When all was said and done the boys were Wednesday fans first, hooligans second. As for the game it proved to be Wednesday's first league victory of the season, thanks to a goal by Tynan. Rumours spread round the East Bank that Jack Charlton was in the North Stand watching the game and had been asked to be the new manager. Tommy could not believe his eyes as Big Jack walked in front of the Kop and disappeared down the player's tunnel. Off the boys shot out of the ground and back into town. Once inside the Claymore the boys discussed the day's events and even the thought of Big Jack being the new manager had not sunk in yet. The group were divided whether or not Jack would take the job. Billy commented that not once all day had the thought of football violence entered the conversation. "If teams changed their manager once a week it would eradicate football violence immediately" he joked. The boys spent the rest of the weekend talking of nothing else than Big Jack Charlton being the Wednesday manager. Over that weekend Jack was appointed the new boss of the Owls, and his first game in charge was away to Exeter, and Tommy was skint. Billy, Bob, Ray, Macca and his mates had booked on the National Express. Tommy had no money for the coach fare so he would try to sneak on the bus without paying. This trick was often done when one or two of the lads had no money. The boys would pile on a coach and make their ·vay to the back and get the young kids to get under the seats. When the driver got up to count the passengers he would always have 52 on board. Once the bus was on its way the youngsters were allowed to get out of their hiding places. On reaching Pond Street two coaches were waiting to take the lads to Exeter. "Shit," Tommy said "They're checking the tickets has you get on" he added. "I told you I'd lend you the money" said Billy. "Now you've blown it cos the coaches are full" said Macca. Tommy faced a dilemma: how was he to see the game? Behind the two coaches there was a car parked up and Tommy recognized one of the passengers, it was a mate of Vinnie's. Tommy knew that they called him Jimmy and he was a member of the Dinnington Owls. "You couldn't squeeze me in could you

Jimmy?" asked Tommy. "What five of us in an Hillman Imp?" he laughed, Tommy was serious. It was the only way he was to see the game. "I can pay for the petrol" Tommy said. "Look, it's not my car. It's my brother's bird's motor" said Jimmy. Jimmy went to ask his brother if there was any chance of fitting Tommy in. Jimmy came back and said they would try it, but if it was too crowded he would be left behind. The first lad, Nigel, got behind the driver, then Jimmy's brother's girlfriend got in, and then Tommy was to sit behind Jimmy. As Jimmy and his brother got in Tommy was praying that they were O.K. Jimmy said it was fine and off they went. He told Tommy that his brother was called Jeff and his girlfriend was Sarah.

It was just over 230 miles to Exeter and they'd given themselves six hours to get there. The little motor was doing good time and, eventually, just after six they reached their goal. The place was buzzing with excitement that this was a new era in the history of Sheffield Wednesday Football Club. The five of them entered the boozer to be met by Billy and the lads. "How was the journey?" said Bob. "A bit cramped but O.K." Tom replied. The party had a couple of beers and made for the ground.

Wednesday had brought a fair following and the team came out to a fantastic reception. Then the man himself, Big Jack, acknowledged the tremendous support. Only one thing was to spoil this special occasion, that was Exeter winning the game 2-1. As the fans left the ground Tommy, Jimmy and the rest headed for the car. It was parked near the bus station and Tommy noticed a group of about twenty following them. Tommy thought this well out of order, twenty wanting to take on four lads and a girl. He knew Jimmy was very handy but was not sure about Jeff and Nigel. Tommy then went for it, marching towards the Exeter mob. "Do you want some of this Sheffield Steel you bastards?" he shouted. Jimmy and the rest were soon backing him up as he was going mental. Tommy had called their bluff. He had just clenched his fist and held out his thumb as though he was gripping something. "The tossers don't wanna know" he laughed.

As the five were about to approach the car three coppers came for Tommy. He was pushed against the wall and told to empty his pockets. "Could you tell me what you're looking for?" he asked the policeman. They told him that they received a complaint that he had pulled a knife on a group of lads. Tommy just laughed. He could not believe that not only did Exeter bottle it, but they went running to the coppers telling tales. Finally the police let Tommy and the rest get on their way home and, sometime after six, Tommy fell into bed. He had booked the day off work and he must have been getting conscientious about his job because a couple of years ago he would have just not bothered turning up.

Saturday saw the Owls visit Wrexham and the boys booked on with Barry from the Lion. Tommy hoped for better luck this time that they would get on the Wrexham end. The previous week in the Harrow Tommy had got friendly with this girl called Jane, who attended Hillsborough to watch the Owls but had not been to an away game. Tommy asked her if she would like to go to Wrexham with the lads, to which she replied, "Yes if you don't mind." Tommy asked Bob to book a place for her when he went to book. "Have you lost your fucking mind?" he shouted. "We don't take women to football." Finally Tommy won the argument and everything was settled. The coach was to leave the Lion at 10am so giving them plenty of time to get to the match. Jane seemed to be excited about her first foray onto enemy soil, and watch Big Jack's lads in action. The lads got there in plenty of time and they went for a drink. While sat in the pub Tommy could sense that the boys were none too pleased with him for bringing the girl along. At 2.30 the boys made their way to the ground to have a go at getting on the home end. Tommy bought his usual programme and paid at the turnstile for himself and Jane. They made their way up the terrace and positioned themselves to the left of the goal. Tommy glanced around and noticed Vinnie's lot had made an appearance. Jane then came out with a peach of a statement: "What colours are Wednesday playing in today?" she said. "Blue and white like they always play in" Tommy replied. "Then why has everyone got red and white on?" she queried. "Because we are on the home end" Tommy informed the shaking wreck. "Look, when the teams come out just make your way to the front, get over the perimeter wall and walk around to the visitors section." This she did immediately and left Tommy on his own. As Tom was watching her on her way Vinnie's boys had made their move on the home supporters, quickly followed by Macca and the boys. Tommy ran to join the lads but the Wrexham fans were heading in his direction, away from the trouble. It was total mayhem, over 200 football hooligans trading blows just for the fun of it.

All the anoraks were safely out of the way and the terrace was left to the gladiators of football. Vinnie stood out with his bright yellow sweater on. Not much chance of him mingling in with the crowd after they had finished. The Police started to restore order and the Owls fans were pushed to the left hand side of the goal where, surprisingly, they let them stay. The rest of the game passed off without incident and Wednesday played out a 1-1 draw. Back on the bus Jane was a bit pissed off with Tommy and told him that was the end of her coming to football with them. The boys gave the poor girl stick all the way home, and that was Jane's first and last outing with the boys.

The following Tuesday saw Tommy return to Doncaster to face the magistrate. He had to be at court by 10am so was up bright and early. Outside the court he met up with his saviour from that terrible night, the lad from Wath who shared a taxi with him. Tommy handed over £5 towards the fare that night and went inside to wait his turn, finally it was Tommy's turn to face the beak and oh shit it was a woman. The charges were read out and Tommy pleaded guilty to get it over and done with. The lady magistrate was none too pleased with our Tom and fined him £75. She asked Tommy how he would like to pay his debt to society and quickly answered £5 per week, "And why was that?" she promptly asked. "Because, your honour, I'm going on holiday in the summer and I've got that to pay for, that plus the money I have to pay my mother." "Holiday?" she snapped. "People like you don't deserve to go on holiday." Anyway, in the end she came round to Tommy's way of thinking and it was paid at £5 a week. Tommy's first brush with the law wasn't too bad after all, but anyone would think that the way the magistrate was talking to Tom that football hooligans were the enemy of the state, and that all those burglars and car thieves don't get fined half as much as Tom.

Tommy made his way home and thought to himself that it could have been worse. Some fans who were getting nicked were paying double that. The rest of the week Tommy just went to work and made up for the lost time. He was working Saturday morning this week because Wednesday were at home to Lincoln and the boys were meeting in the Claymore because they owed the Imps one from last season. They knew that they would bring a few for this short journey and would probably come by train. Once all the boys were together they moved off to the Penny Black. The lads didn't like this pub much because it was usually full of postmen and Unitedites, but it had a good vantage point for the Railway Station.

Once inside the landlord seemed uneasy with the sight of the 50 lads who had converged on his pub. Just then one of Vinnie's mates came in and said that a group of about 200 Lincoln had got off the train and headed up Howard Street into town. The lads quickly supped up and moved back to the Claymore to the landlord's relief. Macca said it was no good trying to find them in town and to head for Hillsborough and settle in a pub on Penistone Road. That would probably be the route they would take to the match anyway. Macca was right and just before 2pm Lincoln were strolling up Penistone Road without a copper in sight. The lads moved out of the pub and the two rival factions faced each other across the busy road. It was a wonder that no one was run down as, in the fighting that followed, bodies were strewn across this busy thoroughfare and the casualties were mounting on both sides. Tommy and the lads were having the upper hand this time, not that they were any better than Lincoln, but the sheer numbers in the boys' favour. But you had to hand it to the Country Bumpkins from Lincolnshire, they were game buggers. The rest of the day was an anti-climax but the Owls did win thanks to goals by Bradshaw and Rushbury.

After the game the boys went back into town to their favourite watering holes where some of the boys were licking their wounds, but not Tommy. This time he had come through it unscathed. As the lads sat talking the subject of their visit to Bradford came up and what mode of transport should they take. The Transit was quickly discarded along with the train. The National were running coaches at £1.50 but they needed to contact Vinnie first and persuade him to organise a coach. The boys knew that Vinnie would be in the Daisy later and, with a bit of arm-twisting, the man would come up trumps.

It was now 2am in the morning and the boys worse for wear had achieved their objective and persuaded Vinnie to run the bus and Billy had stumped up the cash to book them 20 seats "You lot must think I'm a walking bank" he muttered. Tommy had arranged to see Vinnie in the Daisy Wednesday night, not only would they organise the weekends activities but the music was first class and to Macca's and Tommy's liking. Vinnie had some excellent news for the boys. He'd managed to fill two coaches and they would leave from Pond Street at 10am. Tommy asked Vinnie if he had not diluted the strength of their party by going for quantity and not quality. Vinnie reassured Tommy that the boys booked on his bus were not anoraks.

The day of the game all the boys met up in Pond Street and they were all carrying the dreaded newspaper with the spanner inside. Tommy had got his from a fitter at work and it was a real gem. They boarded Vinnie's battle buses to make the short trip up the M1 to Bradford. It was decided that the coaches would drop them near to the ground and they could find some local watering holes. Some of the pubs had their windows boarded up but were still open for business. "I think they're expecting trouble" laughed Willie, as he sipped at his orange squash. Willie did not drink not like the rest of his beer-swilling comrades. He said that drinking and football violence did not mix because you had to be alert at all times and not three sheets to the wind.

Wednesday had brought a massive following, numbering well over four thousand. The pubs and the streets were a mass of Blue and White and there was little sign of any trouble. The boys were growing impatient at the lack of activity and being totally swamped by the anorak and scarf brigades of both teams. They decided to move onto the ground and find some action there. The tight-knit group of over a hundred happy souls marched onto the ground to be met by what seemed to be a small army that was not discriminating between the hooligans and the normal everyday supporter. Anything in blue and white was a target for this mob and the innocent supporter didn't stand a chance. The boys charged at the cowards to see what they were really made of and a full-scale battle ensued. Even the normally placid run of the mill Wednesdayite was joining the lads as they fought with the Bradford hooligans. With the numbers swelled by the normally peaceful anoraks Bradford made a hasty retreat and with the trusty tools safely tucked away it was round one to the Owls. The boys made their way onto the terrace and the section behind the goal was a sea of blue and white. They positioned themselves to the right of the goal, bang next to the Bradford section.

No sooner had the game started when fighting erupted in the Wednesday end. Bradford had infiltrated the Wednesday section and, in the confusion, it was difficult to get the boys together because the anoraks were getting in the way, and all the Bradford lads were top drawer. Eventually order was restored and Wednesday attacked the invaders. Bricks and pieces of wood were being thrown indiscriminately into the Wednesday section and these were being picked up and thrown back. This was the best action the boys had witnessed. Tommy and the lads were at it along with the rest of the Wednesday hooligans trying to repel the Bradford invasion. Bricks were still being thrown from the side section that housed the Bradford supporters into the mass ranks of Wednesday supporters behind the goal.

The police were now on the terrace in force and numerous arrests were being made. Tommy thought that's the last thing he wants, being collared again so soon after his court appearance. But, being a football hooligan, it becomes an occupational hazard. The rest of the game saw fresh outbreaks of violence with Vinnie's party mostly in the thick of it. As for the match that Tommy witnessed very little happened. The Owls got beat 3-2.

Outside the ground after the game the boys gathered together the best they could to have another go at the Bradford hooligans. They wandered the narrow streets around the ground but found little or no resistance. It was as if the Bradford gang had just disappeared into thin air.

The boys made their way back to the coaches and headed back to Sheffield. Tommy sat with Macca and discussed the next big event on the calendar that was Tuesday's gig at the Top Rank. "I've been waiting to see The Clash for a long time" Tommy told Macca. "So have I" came the reply. The rest of the weekend was an anti-climax as far as Tommy was concerned, as he could not wait for Tuesday. Tommy finished work on Tuesday and rushed home like a small boy who was excited about seeing Santa. He was quickly changed and back into town to meet the lads in the Claymore. This was not a football night as you could tell by the turnout in the Claymore. It was a mixture of the finest Sheffield had to offer as far as terrace warfare was all about. But the rivals from Wednesday and United had come together to witness the up and coming youth revolution that Punk was all about. Everybody mingled quite happily and, for the next four hours, they were to witness the best gig Tommy had seen in his life. The Clash were awesome and Tommy was piss wet through when he emerged into the cold night air, steam still rising off his saturated body. Tommy was still on a high when the lads finished the evening off in the Daisy.

Over the next two months not only did Tommy have three home games to finance but also had the visits to Oxford and Gillingham to see to. Crammed into this the boys flitted between the Windmill in Rotherham and the Outlook Club in

Doncaster, and anything the University and Polytechnic had to offer. At the end of it all the boys had seen The Ramones, The Police, The Jam, Ian Dury, The Stranglers, 999, Slaughter and the Dogs and Bethnal, to name just a few. Also Tommy's record collection was growing by the hour, but he had to wait for mum and dad to be out before playing them because it was not everyone's cup of tea.

Wednesday's next big test was to come at Hillsborough on the 29th of November when the mighty Everton were the visitors in the League Cup. Tommy finished work and headed straight for the Claymore to meet the rest of the boys. It was an impressive turn out, not only were the usual boys there but some of their mates that battled for those from the other side of the city were in attendance. The lads numbered over fifty and it was arranged to meet the rest on Penistone Road. It was estimated that the attendance would be over 30,000 and that the Scousers would be well represented. There was just the odd outbreak of violence before the game, but nothing major. The boys all went on the East Bank and Hillsborough, on a big night like this, was looking impressive. Wednesday did not disgrace themselves, finally going down 3-1 to the Mighty Everton.

Before the game had ended the boys made their way to the Leppings Lane end of the ground that housed the opposition. Everton and Wednesday slugged it out and their coaches were being attacked this was becoming a fine end to an enjoyable evening except for the result. The Scousers were trying to defend themselves the best they could, but Wednesday had the superior numbers. Eventually the coppers broke up the fun and forced the boys back towards Penistone Road. The happy bunch made their way back into the town to finish the evening off in the Daisy. Once inside the Daisy, Tommy was met by two mates who went to the Punk concerts with him. They were good lads, even though they both frequented the Lane. Johnny and Tiny could not contain their excitement. "Mort's been on the phone and him and Archie are going to Huddersfield on Thursday to see The Rich Kids" said Johnny. "I don't fancy seeing them, they're too poppy" replied Tommy. "No that's not the reason they're going. You see if you go to see the Rich Kids you can buy tickets to see The Pistols on Christmas Day" Johnny added. Tommy was gobsmacked. The Sex Pistols were finally playing and he had the chance to see them. They were doing a charity gig for the striking Firemen.

The next day Tommy phoned Mort and arranged for him to get him a ticket. It took a few days for the chance to see The Pistols to sink in, and Tommy was on cloud nine. Wednesday were now playing a little better under Big Jack, but the results were still going against them. It was now the 17th of December, the second round of the F.A. Cup and the Owls were at non-league Wigan. The boys had once again gone for Webbo's luxury travel and crammed into the Transit for the short trip across the Pennines. It was ɼlow going and it was further North than the lads had thought, but eventually the travellers arrived and headed for the nearest alehouse. Wigan were expecting their biggest crowd in years, and the boys were expecting a quiet day out and watch a game of football.

Once inside the ground it was quite clear that the Wigan followers had only one thing on their minds; giving the opposing fans a hard time and, at first, Wednesday were not ready for it and the Lanc's had the upper hand, forcing Wednesday to back off. The hardcore of the Wednesday hooligans were finding it hard to group together because all the anoraks were getting in the way. Wigan must have put their team together from all over the North West, because no non-league team has a firm like this, Tommy thought. Once the boys got to grips with the opposition the tide was steadily turning, but both groups were taking casualties and the police were not ready for this outbreak of violence and were finding it difficult to keep the rivals apart. The hooligans were at it for most of the game, which unfortunately the Owls lost 1-0. Tommy could not believe it, fancy losing to a non-league team and what stick would he get at work Monday morning?

The boys walked back to the Transit and one or two were licking their wounds. Once back in Sheffield Tommy had arranged to meet Mort to arrange their trip to Huddersfield on Christmas Day. Wednesday did not have a game until the Boxing Day visit to Tranmere so, for the time being, football took a back seat. He met Mort, Archie, Johnny and Tiny in the Three Tuns. It was a poky little hole, but had a first class jukebox. The talk all night revolved around the visit to Huddersfield to see The Pistols, and where they were going Christmas Eve. Tommy was finishing work next Friday and was not back at work until the 3rd of January.

The boys finished the evening off in the Daisy where they met up with the rest of the lads who had been to Wigan. Around two it was kicking out time and the lads made their way out into the street. They moved along Arundel Gate to make the short walk into Pond Street. It was also kicking out time from the Top Rank and the place was full of all those disco boys who had been on the piss all night. Now, everyone to their own tastes, but a coach full of the bastards from out of town were taking the piss out of Archie's girl because she had bright red hair. See, they thought that because they had the numbers on their side they would take the piss by jumping up and down Punk Style and spitting all over the place. This, the boys didn't mind, but when one manhandled Lizzie, that was it. Now they had the numbers, but the boys had the quality. Willie attacked them full and on so did Macca, Brent and

Archie. Tommy was enjoying this end to such an enjoyable day, apart from Wednesday getting beat that is. Johnny and Tiny were contributing on behalf of the Red side of the city, and the normally placid Mort was giving it his best shot. The bastards were soon cowering on the coach, but that didn't stop Willie pursuing them onboard and finishing one or two off.

With the fun over for another weekend it was time for home and get ready for work Monday. Tommy finished work Monday and headed into town to buy his Christmas presents for the family. Dad was no problem, just aftershave would do. Mother was a bit more trickier but, in the end, Tommy settled on perfume, and Michael was to have the latest Jam album, which was This is the Modern World, only because Tommy had not got that one. Danny was to have a Subbuteo set so that Tommy could also indulge and, finally, Debbie was to have a doll all to herself. With his arms laden with goodies it was off home for his tea and an early night.

Tommy was totally bollocksed after such a hectic weekend and had decided to be totally boring and stop in all week. Tommy managed to survive his hectic schedule and finished work on Friday dinner and went into town to have a drink with his workmates. The first port of call was the Marples, a bit of a dive but his workmates liked it. Tommy was taking a backseat this dinner and just tagging along with the boys. By the time they reached the Golden Ball, which was their eighth port of call, Chris the apprentice was a bit worse for wear. He had got a bit too friendly with this young lady and the boyfriend was not too impressed. The chap wanted to give young Chris a smack for the trouble he'd caused, but Tommy tried to calm him down and settle the matter so nobody got hurt. Tommy liked his workmates, but was not too sure how they would react if Chris got a clip from these youths. This was the last thing Tommy needed; a pub full of drunken revellers and a gang of mates who were, to say the least, inexperienced in the art of causing conflict.

These firm's outings were a pain in the arse for Tommy. He liked the comfort of having the lads round him in case anything kicked off. The youth was adamant that Chris was going to get a smack, so Tommy pulled Chris to one side and told him the situation. "I can murder the tosser" Chris said. Tommy was not too sure. In fact he was certain Chris would be damaged. He told him that if the lad connected with him he should go down, stay down and not to get up. The lads went out of the pub and the youth and Chris got to it. Chris was soon on his arse so Tommy jumped in. "He's had enough" he told the youth. "You've done him" he added. As the rest of the boys helped Chris to his feet the youth wanted more of Chris's blood. Tommy was having none of it and told the youth that the fight was over and his mates were going back in the pub to finish their drinks in peace.

The landlord called last orders just before three and the party finished off their drinks and headed off in their separate directions, not to come across one another until 1978. Tommy got home at teatime and was looking forward to having over a week off work. There was no football until Boxing Day so it was just about having a good time in the pub. Tommy spent the rest of the evening with the family and just chilled in front of the television and had an early night. The boys had decided just to stay local Christmas Eve and not go down town. After a heavy day on the beer Christmas Eve Tommy didn't even make it out at night to his embarrassment and knew he would get stick from the boys.

The family sat around the Christmas tree and young Danny and Debbie were ripping at the wrappings on their presents as if their lives depended on it. Tommy got his usual array of presents; socks, aftershave and a nice sweater from mum. Mick had come up trumps this time getting Tommy the first album by Ian Dury and the Blockheads. With all the niceties over Tommy went for Bob so that they would be in the Royal by 12 o'clock, with mum's words ringing in his ears that dinner is at 2pm prompt. The boozer was packed and all the boys were in. Shess looked nice in his new sweater. Tommy decided to have a game of pool and, while he was bending down to take a shot, Mad Frank poured beer down the nick of his trousers wetting Tommy's pants. Tommy turned round to see Frank laughing his bollocks off. Without thinking Tommy picked up his beer and poured it over Frank's head. The pub went silent as Frank jumped to his feet and headed in Tommy's direction. Our Tom was expecting the worst when Webbo jumped in front of his mate. "Stop there Frank" Webbo told the raging bull. "Can't tha take a joke? Thy started it first and the lads done thi." Mad Frank stood for a moment and than burst out laughing. He was now seeing the funny side and even bought Tommy a drink.

Tommy got out of the pub in one piece and headed home for Christmas dinner. By the time he walked in mum had just finished and was getting ready to serve, dad was carving the turkey and the kids were playing in the room. After dinner Tommy and Mick washed up for mum and tidied the kitchen. It was now 4.30 and Mort was picking him up to go to Huddersfield to see the Sex Pistols. After picking up Archie, Johnny and Tiny it was off to Huddersfield. When the lads arrived at the gig they were met with the sight of the striking firemen who, in the afternoon, had watched the Pistols do a concert for their benefit. "I can't see what all the fuss is about" said one fireman.

When everyone had cleared off from the matinee the boys were let in and, once inside, the lads headed for the bar. With beer in hand the lads took up their position near the front.

94

The Pistols were now on stage and Rotten was wearing a white hunter's hat. He introduced the first song God Save The Queen and the place went mental. No sooner had it started it was all over, the two hours had flown by. "That was unbelievable" Tommy said. The boys headed home because they all had football in the morning and Tommy's lot were at Tranmere.

Wednesday were rooted to the foot of the table and had not won for four games. Webbo took the boys in the Transit and the game passed off without incident. It must be the Christmas spirit, Tommy thought. On arriving home Tommy thought to himself what a wonderful year 1977 had been, not only had his beloved Wednesday got a legend for a manager, but the boys had been involved in some tidy battles to say the least. On the music front he had seen some superb bands and the job was going quite smoothly, so Tommy believed that the year had been good to him, except for getting nicked at Doncaster that is.

Wednesday had started to pick up points but, on the 2nd of January, were beaten at Carlisle. With no game on the 7th Tommy went into town and headed for the Old Blue Bell where he bumped into Webbo's lad, Shaun. The two chatted and discussed what an awful season the Owls were having. Just then a bloke butted in and accused Shaun of having his jacket on. "That coat was stolen out of my car along with my radio" he spouted. Shaun told the lad he must be mistaken because his mother had bought it him for Christmas. The man added that there was an ink stain on the inside pocket and, as Tommy stood there, Shaun opened up the coat to reveal the offending stain. The man was now getting aggressive towards the pair and he must have thought that they were the car thieves. He also had the back up of about six of his mates. Shaun was still adamant that his mother had got it him for Christmas but from where, Tommy thought. The lad wanted his coat back and Shaun was reluctant to give it up. One of the lad's mates came up with the perfect solution: they would head for West Bar Police Station and let them sort it out. With both parties sat languishing in the nick, Shaun's mother eventually arrived to solve the problem. It turned out she had bought it second hand from a shop near Cambridge Street. So off the two parties trotted along with the C.I.D to pay the shop a visit. Once inside the lad was re-united with his radio and, unfortunately for Shaun, his long leather coat. Tommy pointed out to the lad that the toolbox and cassettes belonged to him.

The party left the shop and Tommy headed for the safe haven of his local to finish off this eventful Saturday. Mort came in and asked Tommy if he fancied the Outlook on Monday because this new punk band were playing called Sham 69 and, by all accounts, were pretty good.

The rest of the weekend Tommy didn't do a deal. He missed his Saturday at the match and was back to work Monday morning. Once the work was done Tommy rushed home because the boys were going to the Outlook in Doncaster to see Sham 69. They jumped into two cars and headed for Donny. Along with Tommy and Mort there were Johnny and Tiny plus four lads from the Royal who were mates of Tommy's. They were Alan, Sam, Esso and Mally and they supported United.

Once inside the gig the band were giving away a free single called What Have We Got, which the lads took one or two off their hands. Tommy thought this quite generous for a start. The gig started and the group were on top form and Mort was right, they were good. The band was playing this Saturday at the Polytechnic so after the Owls had been to Swindon the boys were going to the gig. Tommy and the boys had booked on the National and they met as usual in Pond Street. Tommy asked Macca if he was going to see Sham after the Swindon

96

game. To this he replied "Yes, me and about a couple of hundred others." Tommy was the only one out of his crowd that was doing the gig, but Macca, Willie and Brent were going. It was not Billy's or Bob's scene. Mort, Johnny and Tiny were meeting the boys in the Howard along with Esso, Alan, Sam and Mally. Billy was getting a bit pissed off with this music scene. It seemed to be interfering with the football side of things. "Any chance we can put our mind on things in hand, like causing Swindon some grief and not go on and on about bloody music?" Point taken, the lads got settled and planned the day's activities. Vinnie's lot were going straight on the Swindon end and hopefully Tommy's brigade would be joining them.

The coach seemed to take forever to reach Swindon, but eventually the boys arrived at the ground. Straight away they split into smaller pockets and mingled with the home supporters. Tommy bought his usual programme and settled to the back of the kop. As the teams came out it was all-out warfare, with the rivals going at each other as though their life depended on it. Wednesday at first had the upper hand but Swindon had the numbers. Suddenly the boys were surrounded and it was difficult to get grouped back together. The Reds were now giving it to the remainder of fans that were still on the kop, Tommy included. They were ragging him all over the place and he was finding it difficult to stay on his feet. Tommy eventually reached the safety of the pitch, only to be met by two miserable coppers who quickly threw him out of the ground. Lucky for Tommy he was only thrown out and not arrested. There was a small group of Wednesday fans who had suffered the same fate and were just milling around outside.

The turnstiles to the visitors end were now closed so Tommy had to sit out the game on the outside while Wednesday got a credible draw. The rest of the boys took the piss out of Tommy for missing the game and he suffered this all the way back to Pond Street. The lads who were going to see Sham quickly made their way to the Howard where they met up with the rest of the merry bunch. "What have you come as" Tommy said to Esso. "I'm a skinhead now along with the majority who follow Sham" he replied. Tommy was not too keen of the new look that everyone was adopting. He felt that the bovver boy image was not one for your modern day football hooligan, but saying that they did look smart.

Once inside the gig trouble erupted between the skinheads and some students and the boys got dragged into it. When the coppers arrived anyone with a shaven head was singled out and made to line up like on an identity parade. Lucky for the boys they were not involved this time. Sham came on stage and the lead singer was none too pleased with the behaviour of some of the skins. Tommy had come for the music and not for a ruck. After the nonsense had died down the band brought the house down with their lively and energetic set. Tommy was well impressed with these boys from London. "That's the best live act I've seen since the Clash" he told Macca. The boys headed out into the night air and moved on towards town and finished off the night in the Daisy. Tommy thought to himself what a day they'd had; trouble at Swindon, a point for the Owls, Sham were on form and, to top it all, his Auntie was behind the bar.

The rest of January and February saw the Owls improve no end and they picked up 8 points out of a possible 12. Then came March and Wednesday would find it difficult on the park to get a result. The boys had three tasty outings to look forward to. The first was Chesterfield followed by Lincoln and Rotherham, all in the space of 21 days. The lads planned to do them all by train and travel in style. For the first encounter against Chesterfield they were in the town by 10am and, at first, found no trouble at all. This was all to change just after about an hour when they ran into a tasty crew numbering about 50. This lot were more like Mad Frank's age than your average run of the mill football thug. The lads, outnumbered by about 2 to 1, were quickly on their heels. It seemed that for the last two years these country bumpkins had seen enough of their youths getting a good sorting from Yorkshire's finest. They had recruited Dad's Army. The boys played cat and mouse with the codgers all dinner when they stumbled across them having a quiet drink. The plan was to storm the pub and give them grief. Ray popped in first to suss it out and to find out their strength. He had only been gone a few minutes when, suddenly, he reappeared. It was only a poky little place but there were lots of shoppers in. He thought it was a non-starter because it's one thing having aggro but another to involve any innocent biddies.

With the plan changed, Ray walked back into the pub and told the bumpkins that they all fancied sheep to women, or words to that effect. It did the trick and, as they left the pub entrance, they were pounded. They were dropping like flies because they could not get out all at once and the boys had done the tossers. One in particular, with his Amos Brearley sideburns, went down like a sack of spuds. With round two to the lads it was off to the game.

Tommy paid his money and once again entered the home section, but this time Chesterfield were ready and he was attacked straight away. With programme flying through the air Tommy was soon to follow. Anyone who looked out of place was attacked, no questions asked. Tommy got away with just a bloody nose but he was lucky. Some of the lads took a good kicking.

Back outside the ground the lads regrouped best they could, but they were not getting on the kop today. Macca said

"Let's wait until after the kick off then get in." It was agreed that they would try one more time to attack the Spireites. The boys numbered no more than thirty, but at last they were in and together straight up the steps to the left hand side when the chant went up. "Wednesday! Wednesday!..." was the cry and it was battle stations again. The lads made a good account of themselves, but eventually they made a hasty retreat. Bloodied but undeterred they marched onto the side section to watch the rest of the game in peace.

With Chesterfield out of the way for one more year it was next stop Lincoln. This time the boys didn't see much action before or during the game in which the Owls lost 3-1. After the match the boys headed for the town only to be confronted by a large number of Lincoln fans. The two sets of supporters went at it in the High Street, hand to hand fighting sending the Saturday shoppers running for cover. The Wednesday fans gave a good account of themselves before the Police moved in to spoil the fun. The lads moved off in mass towards the Railway Station only to be met by a hail of bricks thrown by none other than a large contingent of Wednesday fans who were probably pissed off by missing the action.

Then, finally, came the boys' Easter showdown with Rotherham. The lads met early as planned and arrived in the Town well before dinner. The place was buzzing with people doing their last minute Easter shopping. The lads numbered about 16 and split into two groups and wandered around the town in search of the Millers. They'd arranged to meet in the Charter Arms just after 12 noon. Tommy's lot were the first to arrive and had only just got served when Macca ran through the door, "Come on" he shouted. "It's kicking off at the bottom of the hill." With the beer left untouched the merry men made their way to join the jollities. By the time the boys had reached the square near the church it was all over. The Police were out in force again. The Police had a lot to thank the hoolies for when sunning themselves on some Mediterranean beach, paid out of all that overtime.

The lads moved on and went into the roughest pub in Rotherham, the County Borough. Tommy had been in a couple of times before, but the lads were only looking for a drink not a fight. Even the Rotherham hooligans gave this place a wide berth. On the way to the pub Ray asked what was it like. To this Tommy replied "Put Mad Frank in the place and multiply him by fifty, that is the County Borough, and that's only the women" he laughed. The boys walked in, bought a drink and settled down to have a sociable drink in the Lion's den.

Gangs of youths were now roaming the town centre and Ray was itching to get involved. He owed them one from a couple of years ago. The plan was to get onto the Tivoli and have some fun with the Millers. As the boys left the pub and made their way to the ground what was happening in the Town did not interest the lads. Their main objective was to get on the home end. This time the boys went in together and did not make the same mistake as at Chesterfield, when they split up. They settled to the left hand side of the goal and it wasn't long before the Millers made their move. I bet they were getting rather pissed off with the Sheffielders taking advantage of their humble abode every year. Fists and Boots were working overtime and the anoraks were quickly getting out of the way. This is where the violence should take place, thought Tommy, and not in the Town and City Centres. Wednesday fans that were spread all over the Tivoli came to swell the numbers. Vinnie was in the thick of things as usual. The Police were finding it difficult to keep the rivals apart and a no mans land was opening up between the rivals. Insults were traded between the gangs, but it was Rotherham's duty to remove the boys from their Kop. Fighting broke out once again and

Tommy was thrown over the perimeter wall by a surly looking copper. As he glanced back in the direction of the Tivoli he could not believe his eyes. The normally placid Mort was giving it his best shot and trading blows in no mans land. Tommy watched the game from the Railway End but could not get over Mort, who was now known as the Terror of the Tivoli.

Wednesday came out on top in this Derby game winning 2-1. The remainder of the 1977-78 season saw the Owls avoid relegation and finish in a respectable 14th place. Things were now on the up for Tommy; his beloved Owls had at last got a manager to be proud of, the boys were going from strength to strength, his job was still suiting him and the music scene was really on top form.

Come and have a go if you think you're hard enough
1978 - 1979

During the early part of 1978 a new club opened in Sheffield. It was called The Limit and it was situated on West Street and it proved popular with the lads. The fixtures were out and, along with the usual battlegrounds, one or two nice ones were added which included Hull City, Blackpool and Mansfield Town. It was now the middle of May and Mort asked Tommy if he fancied The Rafters club in Manchester this Tuesday because Sham were playing. They already had tickets for the Top Rank the following night but fancied a trip to Manchester.

The boys crammed into the Mort Mobile and set off over the Pennines. They stumbled into the club just as the support band was playing. The band was receiving a hostile reception from the crowd. It turned out that they were from Liverpool and that city was not the flavour of the month in Manchester. Eventually order was restored and Sham came on stage and did a terrific set, doing most of their debut album. Things were still a bit hostile so the boys hung around and got chatting to the bass player of the band. Tommy found this strange, rubbing shoulders with Rock Stars, because that's what they were. Their album had reached number 25 in the charts so plenty of people were buying it.

Tommy and the boys eventually arrived home in the early hours and Tommy was meeting the boys straight after work in the Claymore. After work was done Tommy headed for town to meet the rest of the boys. As he walked along Flat Street a mini-bus pulled up and Esso and Mally jumped out. "Come on Tom" they shouted. "The band have invited us to the Hotel." In the bus with the boys were the two roadies and Esso and Mally had been giving them a hand with the gear. Once at the Hotel the roadies introduced the Sheffield Boys to the band. At the gig the boys stood on stage with the band and, once again, the set was terrific. The audience were well delighted with the evening's entertainment and Tommy thought this band was going to be very popular. After the gig the boys headed backstage to rub shoulders with the band. Esso asked the roadies if the band needed a hand with the gear and they were only too grateful that the Sheffield Boys chipped in.

Once the job was done the lads headed for the hotel where they indulged in a few free drinks. The roadies told Tommy that Sham were playing Glasgow tomorrow and Edinburgh on Friday and back to Sunderland on Saturday night. They had a day off on Sunday then it was the Outlook club in Doncaster on Monday. Esso asked Mally and Tommy if they were up for it and, if it was possible to help out the band, would they go. Tommy was dead keen but Mally had a problem. He was due to take his City and Guilds on Friday so Glasgow was a none-starter as far as he was concerned.

Sham gave the boys the green light to join this mini tour so Tommy pissed off home to get into his finest gear and arranged to meet Esso at the hotel in the morning. Mally was pig sick but made the right decision as he had worked all year for these exams. Tommy was up like a lark Thursday morning and caught the bus into town where he phoned work and told them he was sick and would not be coming in. He rummaged through his pockets and pulled out the vast amount of £2.75. That was not a lot to live on for the next five days! On reaching the hotel Esso was tucking in to his breakfast. Tommy was starving but settled for a cup of tea. The roadies told the lads that the band was travelling by train and that they were driving the Transit with the gear and that the tour manager was taking them up with him in the mini-bus. Tommy was overawed by it all and forgot all about him being skint.

The boys made steady progress and reached Carlisle by dinner. The bus stopped outside this large boozer and the party disappeared inside. The Cockneys grabbed the menus and began to browse through it. Tommy asked Esso how much he had on him to this he replied about three quid. Tommy looked at the cheapest thing on the menu which was Chips and Egg. He ordered that twice and two halves of lager, while the roadies were having the best steak money could buy. Once the meal was over Tommy asked how much they owed, to this the roadie replied, "Bugger all. Everything's free when you're on the road." Tommy and Esso were devastated by this news and slumped back to the van.

Finally the party arrived at the Apollo in Glasgow. Wow Tommy thought, what a venue to be playing. But he was soon brought back to earth. Sham were playing Satellite City which was up nine flights of stairs and the lift was broken. The lads put their backs into it and quickly had the gear in place. Soon after the band arrived and did the sound check it was back to the B and B for something to eat. Tommy couldn't believe it, sat at the same dinner table with the band. But, once again, Jimmy put them at ease. With everything sorted it was off to the gig and Sham once again did not disappoint and the Glasgow crowd loved every minute.

The next day it was on to Edinburgh and the gig was all set up by teatime. The road crew along with Esso had to return to the venue to deliver some more equipment. Once at the gig Esso found Mally waiting outside. He had travelled up by train after finishing his exams and was just hanging around outside when he bumped into Esso who brought him back to the hotel. The three mates were re-united and Tommy told him about the chips and egg episode, to which he burst out laughing.

Edinburgh was as good as Glasgow and then it was on to Sunderland on the Saturday. A few more of the boys travelled up from Sheffield, including Tommy's brother Mick, and once again Sham did not disappoint. After the gig Tommy told Mick that he would be home Monday night after the Doncaster gig and to ask Mort to save him a seat in his car to get him home. Tommy was true to his word. He returned home on Monday night and was back down to earth and back at work Tuesday. Esso and Mally stayed on and went with Sham to London. Thursday night Tommy went into the Royal only to be told by the boys that Esso and Mally had just been on Top of the Pops with Sham. They were doing their new single Angels With Dirty Faces.

For the next couple of weeks the boys were enjoying their new-found fame and loving every minute. During that summer the lads went to see Sham at every opportunity at venues up and down the Country. After one particular show at the Roxy in Harlesden the boys were saved from a beating by some Cockney Skins because Vince, a Sham roadie, intervened and told them the boys were his mates. Tommy was very grateful to Vince and his mates because Tommy knew that if it hadn't been for them they'd have got slaughtered. The boys went back to the hotel with the band. Jimmy told the lads that they were not staying the night because they were going home and the hotel was theirs for the night and there was a tab on the bar of which the boys made the most.

Next morning after breakfast the boys decided to hitch home and save the £20 Jimmy had given them all. Tommy and Mally banded together and so did Esso and Alan. On reaching the M1 Tommy and Mally were first to get a lift and were soon on their way North. Esso was getting a bit pissed off with Alan because he was just basking in the summer sun and not taking his turn to try and get a lift. Alan was dozing when Esso finally stopped a van. He jumped onboard leaving Alan still enjoying the sun.

Tommy and Mally arrived home at teatime and were in the Royal by 7pm. Esso arrived soon after and told the boys where he had left Sleeping Beauty. About 10pm the door burst open and in walked Alan. He was none to pleased with Esso and the rest of the lads for taking the piss. Tommy told him it was his own fault for not taking his turn and, by the way, where had he been until this time, he laughed. "I've been travelling around London all day on the tube trying to get a train home" he said. Mally told him that the tube didn't come this far North and the boozer erupted into laughter once again. The episode caused friction between Esso and Alan for a couple of weeks, but soon enough it was all forgotten.

Tommy and the boys travelled to see Sham play at as many venues up and down the country and at one particular gig at the Winter Gardens in Cleethorpes the concert was interrupted by a mob of Grimsby Town fans who were giving the audience grief. Jimmy's patience wore out and it was not long before the West Ham boys were in action sending the Mariners scurrying for the exit doors. Tommy was finding it harder and harder to watch Sham without a major ruck breaking out. It was one thing to have a battle at football but this was bang out of order. Even at the Reading Festival Sham were in the thick of things in sharp contrast to a few days previous when Tommy and the boys went to St Austell and joined the West Ham boys on stage adding backing vocals to the Sham classic Sunday Morning Nightmare.

Tommy spent most of the summer working all the hours he could because this year, along with following the Owls and Sham, the lads had booked to go to Benidorm in October. They flew out on the 10th and were back in Sheffield by the 19th. Tommy and Billy only missed Carlisle and Oxford at home. Along with those two were Alan, Nick and John who were regulars in the Royal with Mickey and Ash who played football with Tommy and Billy. But that was a long way off yet and the new season was nearly upon them.

The boys were ready for another tussle with Doncaster Rovers on August the 12th at Belle Vue. On the day of the game the boys went by train and all the regulars were present: Tommy, Billy, Bob, Shess, Ray, Ian, Chas, Gaz, Terry, Chris, Trevor, Macca, Willie, Brent, Archie and Drum. Wednesday got their season off to a winning start with a 1-0 victory and the day passed off rather peacefully with little or no incidents. Rovers came to Hillsborough the following Tuesday and came away with a 1-0 win, thus meaning that the boys had another trip to Doncaster the following Tuesday. The train once again was the mode of transport and the boys had as usual got together a tidy crew. On reaching the stadium the boys opted for the home section and quickly got about their business and were soon battling with the home supporters. Tommy was more alert this time and kept a watchful eye on the local plod, as he didn't fancy another night in the cells. The action was soon over and Rovers were quickly put in their place, and Wednesday rounded off an eventful evening with a 1-0 win.

After the game, as the boys were making their way back to the town, they spotted an altercation further up the road. Not wanting to miss out the boys were quickly on the scene only to find a group of Wednesday fans ragging about a youthful looking Doncaster fan. Willie was, to say the least, not impressed with their thuggish behaviour and steamed into the gang sending them scattering in every direction. The boys were soon giving him vital support and, I think, really enjoying it. The thugs were soon sorted out and the youth sent on his way no worse for his beating than a bruised face. What would he tell his mates at school in the morning, Tommy thought. The boys were once again on their way when a large group of Wednesday supporters came in their direction, with the so-called thugs in tow. They had gone to get reinforcements to tackle their aggressors. What a laugh the boys had when it was the sight of Vinnie's lot heading their way. "What's all the trouble about then?" Vinnie asked Macca. "Well Vinnie, this lot were doing one defenceless individual and we decided to even it up" said Macca. "And if they want another pop at us feel free" said Willie. With the matter sorted and at an end the boys disappeared into a local hostelry. Alex who came with them now and again was so impressed with the boys' performance that he stood the drinks for the rest of the night because he was always loaded up with cash. Tommy finally got home in the early hours and looked at the clock. Shit, he thought. I've got to be at work in four hours.

Sham had a new single out and it had made the top ten. It was a good tune but Tommy was not keen on the title with it being 'If the Kids are United.' Tommy didn't think Jimmy was singing about the boys at the Lane but Esso said he was. Esso was gloating about this new player the Blades had signed from Argentina called Sabella, but Tommy told him he couldn't be that good or the likes of Liverpool would have signed him.

Wednesday had drawn Aston Villa away in the League Cup and the boys were up for this one remembering that Villa, a few years earlier, had dominated Hillsborough and had swamped most of the ground. Wednesday took a large following and the match ended in a 1-0 defeat for the Owls. After the game Villa came round to confront the visitors but the Owls were ready and fighting broke out at the side of the ground. Villa had numbers on their side and were quickly on top, but it did not help the cause with some Wednesday fans legging it at the first sign of trouble and getting in every ones way. The lads did not disgrace themselves and could be pleased with their showing on the night.

The boys' next game of the season came at good old Lincoln, when the train once again provided the transportation. On the journey to Lincoln the boys were discussing the unfortunate individual who was given three years for a football related crime when, in the same month, someone pushed a pint pot into someone's face and received a fine of just over a £100. The boys thought this harsh to say the least when it was now a worse offence to cause mayhem at football than say burgle or beat up on some old dear.

The boys were soon back on the happy hunting ground that was Lincoln, and were soon trading blows with the opposition. Tommy liked Lincoln, not only would the Imps be up for it once again but the local plod were not too heavy handed. It was now becoming increasingly difficult to infiltrate the home section at Lincoln in any numbers, so most of the fisticuffs were done away from the ground and away from the prying eyes of plod. Wednesday once again were victorious winning 2-1 and the boys went home happy. The Owls were improving with every game and the boys were optimistic that this could be their year.

The next big test for the boys was the visit to Mansfield where, not only had the soccer special been cancelled but the National Coach drivers were on Strike and the normal train service only ran to Alfreton. The boys decided to travel on Friday night and went on the normal service bus. They toured the local boozers and finished up in some grotty little club where Ray pulled this tart who was old enough to be his mother. The woman invited the dirty dozen back to her place where they dossed down while Ray gave her a good seeing too. The next day the lads made their way back into Mansfield where they met up with those who had travelled Saturday morning. The plan was to infiltrate the home section and cause them grief. On reaching the ground the boys managed to infiltrate the home section and quickly got themselves into a tightly knit group. Mansfield didn't take too kindly to this and the boys had a battle on their hands to stem the aggressors. Casualties were mounting on both sides and the anorak brigade were soon making for the safety of the pitch. Tommy was once again using his trusty newspaper and giving it his best shot. The lads had not disgraced themselves against overwhelming odds.

Wednesday had once again made a good account of themselves on and off the field with a notable 1-1 draw. After the game the Wednesday supporters came under a barrage of flying lumps of coal and the boys were finding it difficult to confront the enemy. A mob numbering over 300 had grouped together and were attacking anything in Blue and White. The boys quickly got together and with Vinnie's lot in tow had themselves a formidable force. The 300 were soon dwindled away when they realised the boys meant business and they were soon retreating. The local plod were now making arrests as if they were on piecework. The boys were quickly rounded together and were shown the direction of Alfreton and, with the help of the police transport, were soon at their destination.

The boys arrived in Alfreton and quickly checked on the times of the trains back to Sheffield. As they had a couple of hours to spare they decided to head into the Town and find a boozer. It was not long before the local constabulary were on their case, and they were quickly informed that the boys were only looking for a drink and not trouble. The boys had done their bit for one day and, on looking around, the lads had taken one or two casualties, with Ray and Ian looking a bit battered and bruised. The boys had a few beers then departed for the train and, once back in Sheffield, they headed for the Limit.

Tommy was totally knackered and it was not long before he was heading home to get some kip. Also he needed his money for Wednesday night because The Stranglers were playing the Top Rank and it was £2.50 to get in. The Stranglers by now were into their third Album and Tommy had all three. Also he liked the Band and rated them second only to the Clash. The gig on Wednesday night did not disappoint and all the boys went home happy. By the end of the month the Owls were doing O.K. but had dropped silly points at home to Plymouth, losing 3-2 and drawing 0-0 with Bury, and had also got thumped 3-0 at Swindon.

Tommy was looking forward to his holiday and visiting a foreign country for the first time in his life, but first of all they had to get organised for the visit to Rotherham. On the day of the game it was decided that instead of going to the match early they would drink in Town and set off later in the day. The boys caught the Doncaster bus so avoiding the Town Centre and got off just after Meadowbank. They walked the remainder of the way thus coming to the ground in the opposite direction from the Town. They had quickly dispersed into smaller groups and once again infiltrated the home section and got to it with their rivals. Fighting soon broke out and it was soon realised that the Police were not messing about this time. Instead of containing the situation, they were getting stuck into the rivals and dragging all and sundry in the direction of the exits and throwing them out of the ground thus transferring the trouble from the inside to the streets. Tommy was one of the unlucky ones that made an early exit but, fortunately for him, he was not arrested.

Wednesday went on to win the game 1-0 and Tommy and a few of the lads watched the game from the Railway End with the majority of the Wednesday fans. The boys headed straight back to Sheffield after the game and settled in the Claymore to exchange accounts of the afternoon's altercations. The boys were in total agreement that the Police were on top of things this afternoon, and one or two of the boys never made it to the pub because they'd got their collar felt. Tommy's thoughts now switched to his holiday in three days time, and his trip to Benidorm. The pub was in uproar when Archie came in because his picture was plastered in the local paper being helped by a St Johns Ambulance person at Mansfield.

Tommy and Billy spent Monday doing their last minute shopping and having a drink. Commenting on the season so far Billy said that if the Owls could win the next two home games they would climb the table. Tommy was pleased with himself that he'd scraped the money together to pay for his holiday, and was excited when he met the boys in the Royal Tuesday afternoon.

The boys headed for Manchester Airport to catch their flight to Benidorm. Nick's mum had organised the trip and there was a good mix from kids to the older generation. The flight would be over in a couple of hours, Tommy was reassured. The boys landed at Alicante and the heat hit them immediately. They were staying at the Rio Park and the first thing they did on arrival was to throw the bags in their room and hit the bar. Tommy commented that the lager was shite but it was cheap enough if ever he could fathom out the money. Tommy was sharing with Alan and the first thing next day the boys headed for breakfast. Tommy took one look at his plate and quickly headed for the door. The lads were soon on their way to the beach and were really enjoying the sunshine, but soon got bored so Billy suggested they hired some bikes and for the next couple of hours bombed around the resort locating the local bars.

The boys were soon heading back to the hotel and Tommy was starving and prayed that the dinner would be edible. Billy was not impressed and declined the evening's delights. Tommy just feasted on soup and loads of bread and then followed Billy to the bar. It was not long before the boys were heading out into the evening sunshine.

After visiting a number of British bars the boys entered the Scotsman where they had on sale various sizes of jugs of Sangria. Alan challenged Nick to empty one of the biggest using straws. The boys knelt down and proceeded to make an attempt to empty the liquid through a straw. Nick was first to finish and wobbled to his feet and headed for the toilet. Unfortunately Alan just exploded sending an ugly red liquid in every direction. The lads were hysterical when the barman threw two big buckets of disinfectant over Alan and swept him out into the street. He just laid in the gutter while the angry barman swilled out his bar. Tommy helped the sodden mess to his feet and attempted to help him back to the Hotel. None of the others even raised a finger to help, saying it was his own fault. Tommy could not stand by and see his room-mate in such a state. Eventually he got him back to the room and placed him in the bath. He had to change his own clothes because they were filthy and quickly rejoined his pals. Nick was no worse for his encounter with the red stuff and was soon back swilling down the lager. He was a real beer monster. The lads finished off the evening at a nightclub and finally staggered home in the early hours. The music was not Tommy's cup of tea but he was that pissed that it didn't really matter.

The next day Alan was no worse for the previous nights jollities and, this evening, he had to be better behaved because

Nick's mum had organised a trip to a Medieval Banquet. The boys just chilled out around the pool all day and got ready for the trip that night. Tommy just hoped that the food would be edible and he wasn't disappointed. Also he was having his first encounter with wine but he wasn't impressed. The holiday was flying by and it was over too quickly for Tommy's liking. He spent the last couple of days buying presents to take home and bought his mum and dad a statue of a man forging steel on an anvil and was pretty proud of his acquisition. He also bought Danny a Spanish Football kit. Debbie got another doll and Mick got a dodgy looking T-Shirt.

It was Thursday when the boys arrived home looking rather tanned, and no worse for their sortie onto foreign soil. Wednesday had a game at Shrewsbury on Saturday and Bob had booked the lads on the National. The boys had a good turn out for their visit and Tommy and Billy were telling the boys about Andy's encounter with the red stuff. On reaching the ground the boys breached the home defences but Shrewsbury just weren't up for it. The boys found it a little boring so they watched the Owls fight out a 2-2 draw. Tommy was torn between going with the lads to Blackpool to watch the Owls or going to Glasgow to see Sham at the Apollo and it was also his birthday on that night.

The Owls were now in the top half of the table and Tommy had made his decision and opted to go to Glasgow on the Friday to see Sham and would give Blackpool a miss. This was the first Saturday away game he had missed for over 12 months. Tommy travelled to Glasgow by train on his own because nobody else fancied it. He got to the Apollo mid afternoon while the band were doing the sound check and quickly mucked in and gave the roadies a hand. Sham had now hit the big time and the dodgy Transit was replaced by a big Juggernaut which had all the sound and lighting onboard.

Tommy commented to the Cockney boys how times had changed but Jimmy was the same old person who would always have time for everyone.

The hotel was first class and Tommy was sharing with one of the road crew who was straight on the phone ordering room service. "Please can we have 24 bottles of lager and a plate full of Salmon sandwiches and remember to remove the crusts" he said. Tommy was bent double with laughter when the goodies arrived and the two set about the lager and food. The concert was fine and it was a godsend that they didn't have to hump the gear down nine flights of stairs. Back at the very large hotel the boys set to work mounting up the bar bill which by now was running into three figures. Tommy was well on his way when he eventually hit the sack around 3 o'clock.

Saturday morning the boys headed for Stoke because Sham had a gig on Sunday night at the Victoria Hall in Hanley. The Cockneys were puzzled when Tommy asked to be dropped off at the Railway Station and told them he was heading back to Sheffield to play football Sunday morning. Tommy liked his football and played for the Royal and with Billy being the manager he'd asked him on Thursday if he was playing Sunday, because he was going to Glasgow for the weekend and if he wasn't in the team he'd stop in Stoke Saturday night. Billy told Tommy that he would be playing and it was a cup-tie against the Crown who were two divisions higher than the boys.

As Tommy peered out of the carriage window on his way back to Sheffield he thought to himself that he must be mad missing out on all that free ale that the boys from London are going to consume Saturday night. Tommy arrived home late Saturday to be greeted by the news that Wednesday had done the business in his absence and beat Blackpool 1-0. He quickly had a bite to eat and headed for bed. At 10am the next morning he met the rest of the team and headed for the game. Tommy was playing up front and was looking forward to his Sunday morning football. This was another of his favourite pastimes. The game got under way and the boys were up against it. Not only were the opposition in a higher division but they were top of the league. With the game goalless the boys got a corner and it was swung in for Tommy to get his head to it and hit the back of the net. Ten minutes later Tommy chased a back pass only for the goalie to fumble it and it was 2-0. The boys were playing out of their skin and Billy was like a brick wall at the back. Just before half-time Shess made it 3-0 and the boys could not believe it, and neither could their opponents. The Crown in the second half quickly pulled two back and now the boys were struggling. With ten minutes left Tommy chased a long ball down the left hand side and sent in a lovely cross for Dave to head home to make the final score 4-2 and a place in the next round. Tommy's face was beaming as he left the field and they headed straight to the Royal where he was meeting Alan, Esso, Mally and Brent who were going to Stoke to see Sham.

Tommy was still on cloud nine when he set off for Stoke with the lads. On the way to Stoke Alan noticed a fox that had been left by the roadside and, him being of the hunting and fishing brigade, stopped to see if it was not too badly damaged because if it was not he would have it stuffed. The boys were not impressed with having to spend the rest of the journey with a dead fox.

On arriving at the hotel where the band were staying the Cockney boys didn't look too bad considering their alcohol intake would have been considerable the previous evening. Sham once again played to a packed arena and the boys enjoyed every minute. After the gig the boys made for the hotel and spent the night sinking a very large amount of alcohol. After breakfast the boys headed back to Sheffield and had forgotten about the extra passenger they had onboard. The stink was horrendous from the rotting fox, but Alan would not give up his prize possession.

Wednesday played well up to Christmas and were in mid table, they were still in the F.A. Cup and had been drawn at home to Arsenal in the third round. On the day of the game it was touch and go whether it would be on because the weather had been terrible and early in the week the pitch was covered in snow. But with the help of many fans the pitch was cleared and the match was on. Tommy and the boys gave town a miss and decided to go in Webbo's van to the game because Arsenal did not have a reputation for causing trouble not like Chelsea, West Ham and Millwall.

This was going to be Wednesday's biggest game for just over a year since they played Everton in November 1977. Wednesday played out of their skins and earned the right to a replay at Highbury after the first game finished 1-1. Pat Jennings was pelted with snowballs when he came out for the second half. Tommy decided to stay in the rest of the weekend so he could afford to go to Highbury. British Rail were laying on a Soccer Special to get the travelling fans to Highbury.

Tommy and the lads were on the clock end as the teams hit the field and he was hoping that they would put up a good performance on and off the field because the Arsenal fans were unusually hostile towards them. Was it because of the reception they gave to poor old Pat at Hillsborough? Then the unbelievable happened and Wednesday took the lead and looked like putting out the Mighty Arsenal, until they equalized in the last minute. This really pissed Tommy off and it led to fighting breaking out on the clock end between the rival supporters.

Everyone was subdued as they made their way to the train but the boys had the chance of another go at the Arsenal. The third game was at Leicester City's ground and the boys were going in Webbo's van. It was a squeeze to get everyone in but they managed it. The game was another cracker and at the final whistle it was Wednesday 2 Arsenal 2 and yet another game at Leicester. On returning to the Transit the odd skirmish broke out but the boys were too busy emptying the local off license to get involved. Tommy had now been to three games of football in ten days and his pockets were emptying fast.

The next game was on Wednesday night and Webbo was once again doing the honours. The attendance was well down but who could blame them for not turning up in numbers. This was the second game in three days and they missed a classic as this time it was Wednesday 3 Arsenal 3. The fifth game was on Monday the 22nd of January and Webbo had another van full to bursting but no one ever got turned away. Anyway it was only just over an hour to Leicester.

On arriving at the ground the boys were told that the ground was full and the turnstiles were closed and they were not letting anymore in. Tommy was furious that he had seen all the games so far and he was going to miss this one. The boys moved around the ground and ended up at this big blue gate where the steward had it slightly ajar. He was inspecting tickets of the so-called V.I.P.s who were getting in for free. This really pissed the boys off because they were about to miss this important game. Just then a Wednesday fan ran at the gate and made it fly open. That was it, the boys were in like a shot and Tommy found himself in the main stand. The place was full with all of Football's Finest dignitaries. Tommy sat on a step for a moment and decided to jump down onto the terrace to avoid getting collared if he'd stayed in the stand. He spent the whole of the game alone on the terrace and was livid after the match as Wednesday had lost 2-0. On returning to the Transit the boys were really pissed off with the organisation of the game, but it was soon all forgotten when goodies were brought back from the off license.

The following Thursday the boys from the football team told Tommy that they had drawn the Ship in the next round of the Cup, and Tommy was none too pleased with the news. The boys had played them earlier on in the season and had been booted off the park because the Ship were just a bunch of thugs disguised as a football team. The lads in Tommy's team were not fighters but just a bunch of mates who enjoyed their football on a Sunday morning. If Tommy had his way he would select all the boys from town, but he knew that was just a dream. The thought of Willie, Macca, Brent and the boys tearing round the football field brought a smile to his face.

After the game Sunday morning the boys headed for their local and, as always, they just dumped their kit under the dartboard and headed for the bar. Sat in the corner was Frank and that sent Tommy thinking. He approached Frank and asked if he still had his boots because, in his younger days, he was not a bad footballer. But it was not his skills Tommy was after. He explained that they were due to play the Ship next Sunday in the cup and he was just wondering..... Frank stopped Tommy in mid sentence. "You mean you want me to sort them out?" "Well if you put it like that, yes" said Tommy. Frank agreed to play and I think he was a bit flattered by his new-found fame. Tommy went back to inform the boys about his proposal, but one or two were unhappy about losing their place to Frank. However, Tommy volunteered to step down so Frank could play.

On the morning of the game the Ship were looking as menacing as ever, but how would they handle Frank. Frank took up his position up front as the Ship kicked off and the ball was swiftly kicked forward. As a player ran past Frank they accidentally clashed heads resulting in the player needing urgent medical treatment for his broken nose. Frank was immediately surrounded by the irate opposition, but stood his ground like a good 'un grabbing one unfortunate individual by the throat. Frank informed the Ship that he was here to see fair play and would not injure anyone else if they played the game fair and did not use bully boy tactics like the last time they played. Frank had got his message across and the game was then played in the true spirit that it was meant to be played. The boys ran out comfortable winners in the end and Frank settled down and did all right for a man in his mid forties. Back in the pub after the game Frank was the hero and didn't buy a drink all dinner.

By the end of January everyone seemed to be on strike, except Tommy. Wednesday were after this player called Terry Curran, but Southampton were reluctant to sell. When the Owls played Peterborough at home on the 27th of March they were far too near the foot of the table for comfort, but on a brighter note United were also in trouble. Vinnie was organising a trip to Watford on Saturday and it was then onto London after the game. Even though Tommy was once again broke he was up for it and they'd not had a good trip with Vinnie's lot for sometime.

Wednesday had signed Terry Curran and the talk on the way to Watford was all about this new player. The boys had a fair few drinks before the game and the match ended in a 1-0 defeat for the Owls, but Curran looked good when he came on as a substitute. The coach headed for London straight after the game and Tommy and the boys were looking forward to a night in the Capital. The usual boozers were visited and eventually Tommy and a few of the boys finished up down the Kings Road, made famous by the Sex Pistols, and hung around

Sloane Square for a while. There was a varied selection of Punks, Skinheads and Mods hanging around just posing up and down the road. The boys soon got bored with this and headed for another boozer. Tommy was well out of it when he slumped on the back seat of the coach. He'd really had one too many. As he lay there he could smell smoke and it was getting rather warm. He jumped up to find that he was surrounded by burning newspapers. his mate Oxo thought it would be a laugh to set him on fire, but on a lighter note it did sober him up.

April the 13th saw the Owls visit Hull on a Friday and once again good old Webbo brought out the reliable Transit. Wednesday brought another good following and nothing too exciting happened, to the disappointment of most of the boys. The Owls drew 1-1 with Curran scoring his first ever goal for the Owls. The rest of the Easter programme saw the Owls defeat Chesterfield 4-0 then let everyone down who travelled to Brentford Easter Monday going down 2-1.

The remainder of the 1978-79 season was an anti-climax because everyone was still going on about those battles with the mighty Arsenal. But one thing that cheered the boys up into the summer break was the news that the Blades had been relegated to the third division and the lads at last would get a chance to engage the enemy in a league game and not the dreaded County Cup.

Boxing Day Massacre!
Boxing Day Massacre!
1979 - 1980

The summer of 1979 saw Britain with a new Government after the Winter of Discontent saw Labour replaced by Maggie Thatcher's Conservatives. Tommy was not one bit bothered about politics as long as he had enough money to last him until next payday. He was also not one bit bothered about the state of the economy. He had more pressing problems to sort out like what mode of transport would be taking the boys to Barnsley for the first game of a brand new season on Saturday. They had just had their first battle of this very special season with last Tuesday's visit to Hull, where the Wednesday fans had invaded the pitch to confront the home supporters after the game. Tommy and the lads were in the thick of things and had seen off the Hull lot without breaking sweat. Macca thought it better to travel early to Barnsley and go by train, even though the place would be crawling with coppers. The boys agreed on one thing though, that this would be a great season for those who indulged in terrace warfare. Just glancing through the fixtures saw the Owls having to visit Barnsley, Hull, Chesterfield, Mansfield, Rotherham, Grimsby, Blackpool, Chester, Southend and not forgetting their visit to Bramall Lane.

Saturday could not come quick enough for Tommy. He loved the first game of every football season, especially if the Owls were away from home. The boys met in Pond Street as usual and they had got together a tidy turn out for the visit to

123

the thickies of Barnsley. Once on the train the boys settled back and relaxed on this short journey to Oakwell. On arriving at the station it was clear from the off that the burglars and villains would be having a field day, because all of South Yorkshires Police were in Barnsley having an easy day at the tax payer's expense. Well it beat chasing real criminals the boys thought.

The boys were off the train like a shot and away from the prying eyes of the law and quickly mingling with the people who were out shopping. Soon they had found a nice quiet watering hole and the lads sat chatting and enjoying the first drink of the day. Suddenly, in walked an ugly bunch of youths who were most certainly from Barnsley or some nearby pit village. Barnsley hated Sheffield and everything associated with their fine City. The Tykes knew straight away that the boys were from Sheffield and probably none too pleased that they were drinking in their shit-hole of a Town. Just like Rotherham and Chesterfield they were envious of the Sheffield folk, probably because the loony councillors were spending that much money on hair brain schemes and they were footing the bill. The Tykes engaged themselves in their own little world and gave the boys a wide berth. They finished their drinks and were off leaving the boys once again with the pub to themselves. The landlord seemed uneasy, to say the least, even though the boys had been excellent guests. Just as the boys were enjoying themselves and chilling out back came the Tykes with reinforcements. The boys were now heavily outnumbered and confined to one room. They were sitting ducks. Macca led the charge but there was not enough room to swing a cat and the boys at the front were getting battered. There was nothing the others could do, as the Tykes had got them penned in. Thankfully the Tykes had not resorted to throwing bottles or beer glasses and were only using the equipment they were born with. So, in response, Willie kept his trusty friend hidden from view. Tommy was in the thick of things and giving as good as he was getting. The boys were receiving the worst battering for a very long time, but at no point did any one of them make an exit. They just stuck together like they always did. Eventually the boys made it out of the pub and, with more space to operate in, regrouped together and went on the offensive. Tommy was not keen on terrace warfare invading the Town Centres. He was set in his ways and believed fighting at football should be done in the arena for which they were built and not some service station or Town Centre.

The boys had put up a good show and once again Alex was standing the next round of drinks. They looked a sorry sight when they entered the next boozer but the landlord served them when he saw Alex's wad of money. It was still over two hours to kick off and the lads were once again having a few pints, except for Willie who was once again sipping on his orange. The boys did not encounter any more hostility, mind you, they had done their bit for Club and County for one day.

Once inside the ground there was a tremendous atmosphere, but Ray was having difficulty seeing out of his swollen eyes. Wednesday had once again brought a huge following and did not disappoint for once, running out a victorious 3-0. Straight after the game the boys were that busy celebrating that they got separated from one an other and Tommy found himself with just Willie, Drum and Alex for company as they made their way to the station. Barnsley were now out in force and were after revenge for their players being turned over by those Blue and White Wizards. The four mates stuck together on the walk to the station but all around the atmosphere was turning ugly.

Within sight of the station Drum decided that he needed some ciggies, so the boys detoured into the town to find a shop. With Cigarettes safely purchased the boys headed for the station once again. On reaching the thoroughfare that led to the station a group of youths were milling about at the top. Even though the boys did not wear colours the youths knew Tommy and the lads were from Sheffield. They let the lads past then attacked them from behind. Willie was the first to hit the deck and Tommy, Drum and Alex were finding it difficult to protect their mate. The boys backed off into a shop doorway and Drum was trying his best to drag his mate inside. The Tykes were like animals stamping and kicking at Willies body. Tommy flew at the opposition because his mate was taking a beating and all else did not matter. The onslaught only lasted a few minutes, but to the four it seemed like days. Drum knelt at the side of Willie and could see that his mate was badly beaten. After a few more minutes Willie started to come round and, although his ribs and back were aching like mad, he still managed to ask for one of those bastard fags that had gotten him the beating in the first place.

The boys eventually limped into the station to be greeted by the rest of the crew. Macca was furious that the boys had got themselves separated like that and had took such a beating after putting up such a good showing earlier in the day. As the boys made it back to the safe haven of the Claymore they reflected on the day as a whole and, apart from Ray and Willie, the rest did not seem too bad. The boys finished the evening off in the Limit and planned a hostile reception for the Tykes when they were to visit Hillsborough.

The music scene at the time was very vibrant with the emergence of the Two-Tone bands such as The Specials and Madness along with Sham, who had just released Hersham Boys. Tommy told Esso that it this was going to be called

126

Wednesday Boys but Jimmy thought it would upset the boys down West Ham too much. The Clash were still busy turning out records along with The Stranglers so the Punk scene was still going strong.

Wednesday had made an excellent start to the season and after victories against Barnsley and Plymouth in the League and Hull in the League Cup they let us down with the home defeat to Blackburn. Wednesday were none too pleased with the behaviour of some of its supporters and came out with the statement 'Hooliganism is not Wednesdayism' which brought a smile to the boys' faces.

Tommy had bought his season ticket for the vast sum of £21.50 which would save him £6.10 over the season. After drawing at home with Manchester City in the League Cup the Transit was put to good use for the replay on the 4th of September at Maine Road. The boys climbed on board for the short journey across the Pennines and just made it for kick off. City had an impressive following home and away and the boys knew they would have to stick together like glue after the game because City would certainly come to brawl after the match. With eight minutes left Mark Smith put us in front and thoughts turned back to that great night at Wolves a couple of years ago. But it was not to be with City scoring twice to win the game 2-1.

On leaving the ground City came at the boys and they were being pushed in the totally different direction from where the Transit was parked. Fists and boots were being exchanged at an alarming pace and the boys were standing their ground. They were totally outnumbered and so they made the decision to make an organised retreat and not get split up. The boys found themselves in a maze of back alleys it was just like Coronation Street, laughed Billy, just to ease the tension that was creeping in. The boys eventually made the decision to head back in the direction of the ground and find the Transit. Gangs of youths were everywhere and the boys found it uneasy but knew if it kicked off the lads would fight it out even though they would probably come second. Moss Side was not a pleasant place at the best of times, especially if you were white and not familiar with the surroundings. But the boys plodded on regardless and had never been so relieved to see that battered old Transit sitting there it all its glory.

So the 1979-80 season was only a month old and the boys had encountered trouble at Hull, Barnsley and now Manchester City. The bad behaviour of the Wednesday supporters had not been confined to the East Bank. The old codgers in the North Stand had been deprived of their cushions after hurtling them onto the pitch during the 3-0 defeat at home to Blackburn. Even Unitedites had been acting up and when returning from a game at Doncaster. Esso and his mates had been thrown of the train as the transport police terminated the train at Conisborough, leaving the Reds stranded miles from home.

September the 29th saw the boys get ready for yet another visit to Chesterfield. The tussles with the country bumpkins were, to say the least, thin on the ground these days. The police were largely on the ball to keep the rivals apart. The lads arrived in the town quite early but found no problems like they had encountered on previous visits. They spent the day wandering round the town just having the odd glass before the game. Wednesday were beaten 2-1 thus capping off a miserable day both on and off the field. The boys headed back to Sheffield and made for the Claymore where they met up with Esso and his mates for a drink around town and then hit the Limit. While the boys were having a quiet drink in the West Street Hotel a Unitedite, who was known to the boys, came in and was looking for trouble from the start knowing that the boys frequented the Blue side of the City. Tommy was a bit pissed off with his threatening attitude because he believed that football terrace activities should be left where they belong, on the terrace. Tommy had never had any trouble with this Wednesday versus United shit because a lot of his music and socialising friends visited the Lane. On the odd occasion when the boys had tussled on the Shoreham with the Blades he found it odd that for 90 minutes he was trying to do damage to the people who he'd be drinking with a few hours later in the Limit.

The Blade now was taunting the boys that he had a mob of 50 to hand and that they would murder this lot. To this Macca replied "Well bring them in then tosser." He quickly turned to Esso and his Mates "You're Blademen arn't you?" To this Esso replied "Not at this present moment in time." The Blade was now taken aback with Esso's reply and made for the door to join his cohorts on West Street quickly followed by the boys. The lads quickly confronted their opponents. Tommy found it strange because he got on quite well with most of them and didn't feel it right that it had come to this because of one mouthy individual. Macca then came up with a face saving solution because the Blade had put both sets in a no win situation. Tommy knew that neither side would back down and this put Esso and his fellow Blades in an awkward situation. Macca challenged the gobshite one on one there and then, nobody else getting involved. The Blade was reluctant but could not back down in front of everyone because he towered above Macca. What the boy lacked in height he made up for with bottle, by the crate full. Macca flew at him and in no time the mouthy shit was not so mouthy any more. This had set a dangerous agenda because by the time the story had been circulated around it would have been blown all out of proportion with the gobshite telling all that he'd been done by a mob of Wednesdayites and not just Macca. The boys finished the night off in the Limit in peace and listened to the good music.

Wednesday had chartered a train for the trip to Hull on Tuesday the 9th of October after the success with the Arsenal games and said that if it was popular they would repeat it. Anyway Tommy thought it was more comfortable than the Transit. The visit to Hull was a success and Wednesday came away with a point. Football violence was now getting out of hand and the magistrates were getting tough. The fines were ranging from the hundreds to 3 months jail. On the 6th of October United visited Rotherham and the perimeter wall collapsed injuring quite a few people. The press had a field day and called for Millmoor to be closed down as Wednesday were due to play there the following Saturday. Esso and his mates were in the thick of things at Rotherham and boasted that it was the worse violence that Rotherham had ever encountered. To this he was quickly put in his place when Macca told him that Wednesday had been sorting them out for years.

On the day of the game the boys travelled late to the game thus avoiding the large police presence and arrived in very small numbers. It had been arranged that they would all meet up on the Tivoli End and some of the lads had invested 85p on a Rotherham silk scarf to gain access to the home section. Tommy had travelled with Billy, Bob and Chas and entered the ground about 2.45 and not a drop of beer had passed their lips. They quickly teamed up with the rest of the boys, some still sporting the colours of Rotherham. Tommy commented that it was like a home game with the amount of Wednesday fans inside the ground. The game had only just started when Mullen scored and the Tivoli End erupted and the boys swiftly got rid of the Rotherham colours and set about engaging the enemy, thus causing supporters to panic and spill onto the pitch. The police were having difficulties keeping the rivals apart and when Rotherham levelled the Millers surged towards the Wednesday fans that remained on the kop.

Fighting was now at its peak and the boys were in the thick of things and one or two were being led out by the police. Just before half time Curran put Wednesday back in front to the delight of all the boys that remained on the Tivoli. During the interval the boys decided to obtain refreshments from behind the terrace and were soon exchanging blows with their rivals once more. The wall had once again given way and the place was in chaos, but the Owls were winning and that's all that mattered. Tommy and the boys were jubilant as they headed for the bus station and were once again being put to the test with the Millers coming at them from everywhere. As always they stuck together as one and Rotherham were soon backing off and going in search of easier prey than these battled hardened terrace warriors.

With the day's work done it was back to Sheffield and to indulge in the finer things like drinking and more drinking. The boys had earned it and Alex was once again putting his hand in his very wealthy pockets. By the time Grimsby were the visitors to Hillsborough on the 23rd of October the Owls were in 5th place, but the Blades unfortunately were top. With the success of the train to Hull the club had now decided to run two more to Grimsby on the 6th and Blackpool on the 10th of November. With the price being affordable the boys had decided to use the train to these games. Tommy had organised with Mort to hire a box van for the trip down to Wimbledon because their old pal Mick was now living in Didcot, just off the A34 on the way to Oxford. The boys had arranged to borrow the landlord's benches that he put out in his beer garden in the summer so the boys would be comfortable on the long journey South. Tables were also commandeered so that cards could be played to pass the time by. It was also agreed that this would be a violence free trip because some of Mick's old mates were of the anorak and scarf society and were along just for the piss up and to see an old mate.

There were well over 20 in the party when the van set off for Wimbledon and everyone was in a boisterous mood. Not only was it match day once again but Wednesday were on a roll and the drink was flowing inside the van. This was the first time that the boys had used a box van and everyone commented how it was better than the Transit, but not to let Webbo know because it might hurt his feelings.

Wimbledon was soon awash with thousands of Wednesdayites and not a sign of any trouble. The game was unbelievable and with Wednesday sporting an all white strip like the mighty Real Madrid, Wednesday went 1-0 through Lowey. Then it was 1-1 until Curran made it 2-1 to the Owls. Just after half time the Dons drew level but Smith from the penalty spot put the Owls back in front before Curran made it 4-2. In the last minute Wimbledon scored to make the final score 4-3. The boys were in a celebrating mood as they followed Mick back to his village and the landlord thought it was Christmas when the boys marched in to the pub. Mort had a subdued look about him because he had to drive this lot home later. This was the happier side of following the Owls away from home and Tommy and the boys enjoyed these occasions as much as the times when they were engaging the rival supporters. The day had flown by and Tommy told Mick that the next time the Owls were in the area they would do it again. To this Mort said "But I'm not driving."

The following Saturday saw Barnsley visit Hillsborough and after such a peaceful day at Wimbledon it was back to the real world. The boys wanted revenge for the beating they took after the game at Oakwell. The normal football supporter had

132

nothing to fear from the boys. It was the Barnsley Bootboys with their NCB donkey jackets and pit boots that did the damage at Oakwell, and the boys knew where to find them.

The lads had quite a large turn out when they assembled in the Claymore and were quickly heading in the direction of Hillsborough, settling in a pub on Penistone Road. The boys banked on the Barnsley hooligans travelling by the normal service train to Sheffield then walking along Penistone Road to the ground. Willie was really up for getting revenge for that day in August and the boys had to stop him from going back towards Sheffield because he was growing impatient waiting for the Barnsley to arrive. At about two o'clock a small gang of youths smartly dressed in their finest NCB clobber wandered nervously along towards Hillsborough. Macca led a small group out of the pub and quickly got in front of the Reds and engaged them in combat. Willie was at it like ten men and was dishing out what he received back in Barnsley. The Barnsley fans made the mistake of running away from the ground and back into the direction of the pub, where they were met by another onslaught from the rest of the boys. It was now becoming too one sided but the boys remembered the state some of the lads were in back in August. One or two of the Reds had taken a bit of a beating but if the boot was on the other foot they would have done the same. As for the match the Owls lost 2-0.

After the game the boys headed into town to have a few beers and reflect on the afternoon's activities. The talk was about Sunday's concert and the chance to see The Specials, Selecter and Madness on the same bill. Two-Tone was becoming very popular amongst the boys, more so than what Punk had been. Tommy thought it was because the dress was more in line with the Mod look of the 1960s and it appealed to the more fashion conscious of the group. Sham were also having difficulty playing to a trouble free audience after all the violence at the Reading Festival back in August. The boys had not seen Sham play for quite a while. At this point Trevor came in and told the boys about his conviction at Rotherham that led him to receive a £500 fine. He was having difficulty paying it and was having the wife giving him grief about going to football. But, as always, Trev had the answer to his problems. First he would get a job then get shut of the wife. The room just burst into laughter. Tommy knew Trevor was only jesting because he would never get a job even if his life depended on it.

The boys met early on Sunday and were in the Top Rank as soon as the doors were open. Selecter played a steady set and Madness were outstanding, but it was the boys from Coventry who stole the show. The Specials were awesome and had the place heaving to their special sound and Tommy would be adding another band to his ever-growing list of bands to follow.

Wednesday finished November riding high in the league and with the success of the chartered trains things were now looking up for all Wednesdayites. The lads decided that the train was now their number one form of transport and Tommy thought it was reasonable at £2.60 to Chester. Also it arrived in time for the boys to get a drink. Because Chester did not have a reputation for causing grief, the boys settled back and enjoyed the trip to the game. Tommy, Billy, Bob and Chas indulged themselves in a game of cards and the only thing that was missing was the beer. The Owls sent the boys home happy with a 2-2 draw.

It was now fast approaching Derby day with the forthcoming visit of Sheffield United to Hillsborough on Boxing Day. The 11am kick off was not to the boys liking because it interfered with their usual match day ritual of having a quiet drink then rushing to the game just in time for the kick off. The usual Wednesday versus United banter between the friends was becoming more hostile as the day approached but, as the Owls had the upper hand on the violence front, it never got out of hand. Esso was still bragging that the Blades had the better team and that the Blades would make a show on the East Bank on Boxing Day. Tommy knew this was just a dream on Esso's part because every time the Owls had visited the Lane the boys had routed the Blades with ease. Non more so than over a year ago when the boys had met in the Claymore and headed for the Lane in the dreaded County Cup. Wednesday had a good turn out and waited until the last minute before heading for Bramall Lane. As the lads approached the ground a chant of "United" went up and some Unitedites joined the boys. Once inside the Blades just stood there because they had been informed that Wednesday would be making a showing tonight. Once all the boys were in Tommy showed his true colours to the amazement of the startled Reds. Up the staircase the lads charged and straight across the Shoreham to face the enemy. Tommy was soon in the thick of things but so was Esso and Mally for the other side. Wednesday were just too strong for the Shoreham Boys and soon had them on the run, to the disappointment of most of the boys. The police just contained the situation but it was over too quickly, after all the boys had done to organise it.

On the day of the Derby game Tommy was up bright and early and baiting Mick that it was a waste of time him turning up because the outcome was inevitable. The brothers left for the game together as Webbo was taking the Transit. All the boys from the local jumped on board and headed for the game, Wednesday and Unitedites together. The banter was friendly enough between the mates and they knew, whatever the result, they would return to the pub together. Mick and the rest of the

Blades headed for the Leppings Lane while Tommy and the boys headed for the East Bank to see if the Blades had dared to infiltrate the Kop, but not a one had shown their face.

The stadium looked fantastic with nearly 50,000 inside and both teams came out to a tremendous reception and not a sign of trouble anywhere inside the ground. The game was a tense affair and Tommy was hoping for the right result after waiting a long time for this. His prayers were answered just before half-time when Mellor sent a screamer into the goal in front of the Kop to send the Wednesdayites crazy. The half-time refreshments tasted so much sweeter for Tommy and the boys and they could not wait for the second half to get underway. On the hour Terry Curran headed home in front of all the Unitedites and proceeded to kneel in front of them sending them crazy with rage. But this sent the rest of the ground into a Blue and White frenzy of untold joy. Tommy had just got his breath back when Jeff King slotted in number three and the place was unbelievable, especially if you happened to be a Wednesdayite. When Tommy thought it couldn't get any better Mark Smith ended the massacre with number four from the penalty spot.

The boys poured out into Penistone Road and celebrated like never before. Tommy had not witnessed anything like it in all of his 15 Years of being a Wednesdayite, and the rest of the day would for him go too quickly. Back at the van there was no sign of Esso and the dejected Blades. Probably they had all jumped in the River Don, laughed Chas. Only Mick turned up for the trip back to the Royal and Tommy started to feel sorry for his brother, but then remembered all the stick he had dished out over the years.

The pub was totally Blade free when the jubilant Owls marched in to celebrate. But the celebration was short lived when the landlord shouted last orders and emptied the pub.

136

Tommy hated the draconian licensing laws after sampling the delights of being able to get a drink in Spain at anytime of the day or night. The boys would be back in the pub later and would finish the evening off in the Harrow and would be worse for wear come closing time. As Tommy and the boys sat having a drink in walked a dejected Esso with a face like thunder. But that did not stop the boys giving him grief. As the boys sat round enjoying every minute you could count the Unitedites on one hand.

Tommy was still on holiday but could not wait to give the Blades grief at work after the New Year. The New Year celebrations were at an end and Tommy was back at work. He was one of the lucky ones because the jobless were increasing by the day. Wednesday were on a roll and, by the time Colchester were the visitors to Hillsborough, the Owls were 6 points off the top with 3 games in hand.

The month of February saw the Owls win 5 times and draw against Chesterfield at Hillsborough 3-3 thus putting them in the top two. Tommy could not believe it. Wednesday were only 13 games away from gaining promotion.

Tommy was up bright and early Monday morning and he was off to work to give those Blades some stick. Once he'd clocked in he headed for the canteen to make a brew. The canteen was like a morgue and Tommy could not believe what he was hearing, that the factory was closing forthwith and making over 100 people redundant. "I can't believe this is happening to me again," shouted Tom. Everybody received a letter telling them that due to the state of the economy the factory was no longer viable because the manufacturing industries were in decline. Tommy was told that his money would be waiting for him Friday, and so off he went home to break the news to his mother. Tommy was totally pissed off with everything and could not believe he was once again on the dole. Wednesday were having such a tremendous season he knew something would come along and spoil it.

Thursday night Tommy was having a drink in his local when Alan walked in. He'd heard that Tommy was out of work and suggested that the two of them should bugger off to Jersey. He told Tommy that his mates were over there and there were loads of jobs to be had. Tommy was tempted but what about his football and music and socialising with the boys? He would miss all that, he told Alan. After a few more beers Tommy said he would give it a go and the lads decided to collect Tommy's redundancy and book to leave on Monday. So Tommy had one last game which was the visit to Oxford United on the 1st of March.

The boys had decided to travel on the Inter-City Owl. Tommy was a bit down beat but enjoyed the day out and Wednesday sent him on his way with a 2-0 victory. Monday came and the boys set off for Jersey, eventually arriving Tuesday night because the woman in the travel agents had cocked up the travel arrangements. There was no sailing late on Monday evening out of season, so the boys had to find a bed and breakfast hotel. They were joined by Esso's brother who had flown out Monday and he knew the ropes and soon found the trio some digs. It would cost them £27 a week between them, so Tommy thought that was reasonable.

Alan and Steve got a job straight away because they had a driving licence but Tommy didn't. The job involved cleaning hire cars at the airport. Tommy was finding it difficult to get a job but, by the end of the month, Steve's boss had arranged for Tommy to help his dad with some odd jobs. Tommy enjoyed his job and walked to work each day along the sea front. Tommy liked Jersey but missed Saturday afternoons like mad. He would phone Billy without fail every Sunday. The lads would go for a drink every night but not once did Tommy fail to turn up for work. Charlie his boss paid him £60 a week which was ample to live on.

Wednesday were now sitting pretty in the top two and with the Derby game looming in five days time Tommy was getting homesick. On the day of the game the boys hit the Red Lamp as usual. Tommy, Steve and Johnny were gunning for the Owls and Alan and Fred were rooting for the Blades. The boys were hitting the beer like it was going out of fashion. Tommy was thinking about all the boys and if they were having any trouble. By the time the results came on the honours were even with the result being 1-1 with Curran, according to all reports, scoring a wonder goal. But the boys had a few more hours to go before they could see it because the game was to be shown on Match of the Day. Tommy was well pissed when they cleared the Red Lamp so they could tidy it up for the evening session. He and the boys headed for some tea before setting about the beer once again. By the time the Match came on Tommy and the lads were out of it but it didn't spoil them enjoying their own personal Derby Day festivities, to the amazement of all onlookers, with the various chants in support of Wednesday and United.

The lads finished the evening off in the local nightclub and Tommy was surprised to see how friendly everybody was to one another, even though they all came from all the major cities in the U.K. including London. The boys' local was the Red Lamp and if anyone was down on his or her luck and jobless the bag would be passed round and the money handed to the said person. Tommy was on the receiving end of this practice after he had been in Jersey for four weeks, and still jobless. He had stayed in one Saturday and everyone was enquiring where he was. Steve told them that his money was running out and he was giving this Saturday a miss. The bag was passed around and the proceeds handed to Tommy via Steve.

Tommy enjoyed the island life but missed his football, Wednesday were on top form and even after they had lost to Bury 1-0 they were still second. But Blackburn and Chesterfield had both got a game in hand and Rovers were level on points with Chesterfield two points adrift. On the 19th of April the Owls beat Chester at Hillsborough 3-0 to set up Tuesday's visit to Blackburn as a 'winner takes all' encounter. Tommy finished work and headed for the digs where Steve was already waiting. The lads had decided to hit the Red Lamp and the beer in anticipation of Wednesday doing the business. The boys knew that defeat would probably result in the Owls having to endure another season in the third. They sat drinking all night and the waiting for the result was a nightmare, but it was all worth it in the end with the Owls running out victorious by 2-1. The boys finished the evening off in the nightclub and everybody was asking who's birthday the boys were celebrating. They replied "Big Jack's." The punters spent the rest of the evening trying to locate Big Jack to buy him a drink.

Tommy was in a right state when he went to work and told himself that he would be home before the new season started. Even if it meant being out of work and on the dole he missed his football too much. The season ended on a high for the Owls who gained promotion to the second division and Tommy was true to his word and travelled home on Cup Final day, the 10th of May 1980 to seek out employment back in Sheffield.

The boys are back in town! 1980 - 1981

The summer of 1980 saw Tommy get back onto his feet by obtaining employment at an engineering works just off City Road. The money was not good, but he didn't have to work Saturdays. On the music scene the boys had been to see Sham play at the Glasgow Apollo with the two remaining Sex Pistols. Nothing came of said merger between the bands, only that the Sheffield Boys had their name mentioned in the music press. The boys had seen The Undertones and The Clash were still turning out great records. But the main reason why Tommy had returned from Jersey was that he missed watching Wednesday play.

The Owls had once again sorted out United on and off the field with victory in the League Cup, but now would come the first test of the season at home to Newcastle United. The boys were still together; Billy, Bob, Chas, Terry, Trevor, Gaz, Archie, Shess, Ray, Willie, Brent, Drum and Macca. When the boys met in town it was just a sea of black and white everywhere they went. The majority of the Geordies were just on the piss but the boys had all ready encountered a gang of hooligans and it was only 11.30am. The boys knew they would be up against it today because the higher you went in the league the stronger the hooligan element became. Wednesday were expecting a crowd of nearly 30,000 with a large following coming from the North East. The boys knew what to expect after United's encounter a couple of years ago. Tommy and the boys headed for the Complete Angler to be met by the landlord and his big dog. He let the boys in and it was a Geordie free zone. All the pubs were closed around the ground so the lads decided to stay in town. The Old Blue Bell and the Golden Ball were shut, so the lads headed for West Street. Newcastle were everywhere when the boys eventually decided to head for Hillsborough. Macca was hoping that the boys would meet up with Vinnie's lot for the afternoon's festivities.

On arriving at the ground the boys entered the East Bank and were soon at it with those black and white invaders and boots and fists were flying towards the Geordies. Tommy was back where he belonged, at Hillsborough on a Saturday afternoon with his mates. The boys had Newcastle penned at the bottom of the Kop and fighting was now breaking out in the North and South stands. The season was back with a vengeance and the boys were busy protecting their sacred ground. The lads were now getting to grips with some of the worst hooligans in the U.K. and were holding their own.

Wednesday did not let the boys down running out victorious 2-0. After the game the police held the Geordies in to allow the Wednesdayites to get organised for the long walk back to town. Most of the Newcastle fans had come by coach and were quickly dispatched on their way, but still a large enough mob were heading in the direction of the city, towards the Railway Station. The lads were soon engaging the enemy and had the element of surprise in their favour, with being on home soil. Town seemed deserted with most people staying local until the Geordies had gone home, but the boys headed for West Street to finish off what had been a very long day.

The papers were full of the trouble on Monday night and Tommy's dad was giving him grief about 'those football hooligans' as they sat having their tea. Tommy let it go over his head and just agreed with all that his dad was saying until he'd finished his tea. Then he was upstairs to listen to his music.

The Owls had a game on Tuesday at Bolton and would be taking a fair following, even though it was a night game. The lads got Webbo organised to take them in his brand new Transit which was ten times better than the old one. The ground was packed with Wednesdayites and, as usual, they were crammed in like caged animals. "No wonder there's trouble when they treat us like this" spouted Billy. The Owls fought out a 0-0 draw to send the lads home happy, that was when the Police finally decided to let them out.

The following Saturday the same happened at Notts County. The supporters were penned into one section of the terrace when there was space all around. This was really pissing the boys off, this and the fact that Wednesday were getting beat 2-0. But they could not engage the enemy today as County didn't have any hooligans, not like their neighbours Forest.

The end of August saw the boys getting piss wet through on the East Bank watching the Owls demolish Preston 3-0. Tommy was enjoying his new job even though the money was shite, but his workmates seemed O.K. Dad was still in the same old job and Mum had still got her part time bar job. Tommy was now 25 and his mother was always going on about him settling down and not hanging around with the boys. Mick was 20 and still a shitty Blade, but Young Danny, even though he was only 11, was a conscripted Blue like Tommy and his Dad. Little Debbie was still undecided where her loyalties lay.

The week flew by and it was soon Friday night and the lads were on the Town celebrating Ray's birthday. The talk all night was about Saturday's trip on the Inter City Owl to Oldham and the Owls were taking another large following.

Tommy was hoping that they would not be caged in like they were at Bolton and Notts County. The boys had enjoyed their night out and were heading down the Moor when a couple of the youngsters got into some bother with a gang of youths. Before they knew it Tommy and the boys were going at it hell for leather and had soon dispersed the mouthy rabble. Tommy glanced round to see Bob laid on the ground, unable to move. The lad had damaged his leg and could not move it. The ambulance was soon on its way to hospital with Bob inside and that put a right dampener on the evening's jollities. The boys were soon wending their way home.

First thing Saturday morning Tommy was round at Bob's to enquire if he was in, only to be told by his mother that he was not home. Tommy informed the good lady that her son must still be in the hospital, bid her a good morning and rushed to tell the rest of the boys the news. It was unfortunate for Bob, especially has he had a ticket for the match. But the boys would be thinking about him as they were hitting the beer.

The train was well organised as usual and not one bit of bother were the fans causing, not like the dark days of the soccer specials that used to get smashed to bits. The Inter City Owl was different because the fans policed it themselves, plus the boys detested mindless vandalism. At the railway station the fans were herded onto buses for the final leg of their journey. Tommy was none too pleased with the way the police were manhandling the visiting supporters. "Every time Wednesday take a large following anywhere the police just cannot contain the situation without resorting to their bully boy tactics" spouted Shess.

Tommy and the boys were soon sampling what Oldham had to offer and all the pubs were quite busy. Macca informed the lads that Vinnie's lot had requested their presence on the Oldham end and the boys truly obliged. It was 2.30 when the

144

lads entered the Oldham Kop and were soon at it with the Oldham hooligans. But the boys had underestimated the resistance from the Lancashire Tosspots. Macca was none too pleased that the lads had been shown the door but, then again, what can a mere 20 do against a terrace full of mindless thugs. The boys had not organised themselves enough and were well short on numbers when entering the home section, so settled on having a further go after the match. Billy commented that these fences were a disaster for the hooligans because it took away the escape route onto the pitch if they found themselves heavily outnumbered. The Wednesday fans were penned in behind the goal opposite the Oldham end and had brought another large following. The boys settled down behind the goal but there were still outbreaks of violence coming from the Kop end. "If we had got better organised before the game we'd still be over there" said Macca. The boys agreed with him entirely that the communication between themselves and Vinnie's boys was a total disaster.

The teams came out to a tremendous reception and the boys saluted their former hero Rodger Wylde, who was now playing for the opposition. The game was evenly balanced, but then Oldham went in front just after ten minutes. Just before the half hour mark Curran and Stainrod got tangled up together and Curran was sent off. The Wednesday fans went mental throwing anything they could lay their hands on in the direction of the pitch. Fans were trying to scale the fencing to get onto the pitch. The referee had taken the players off to the safety of the dressing rooms and even Big Jack could not curtail the explosion of violence. Lumps of the terracing were being used as missiles and aimed at the police. Tommy had never seen anything like it. The Wednesdayites were totally out of control. The boys took a back seat and just watched from a distance. The throwing of objects had not been a favourite pastime of the boys. They preferred to engage the enemy toe to toe. After about half an hour order was restored and the game continued resulting in a 2-0 defeat for the Owls. The boys, together with Vinnie's mob, confronted Oldham outside the ground and this time the battle went like clockwork. The lads had soon dispersed the enemy to the joy of everyone involved.

The boys were well behind schedule when they alighted at the Midland station and the police were out in force seeking retribution for the way their colleagues over the Pennines had been treated. The boys headed straight for West Street where the talk all night was about the Oldham riot. Tommy knew for well that he was going to get grief at home, even though he was not directly involved in the trouble.

The following weeks Wednesday were never out of the papers and the F.A. banned all Wednesday fans from attending the games at Derby, Grimsby, Swansea, and Bristol Rovers, plus the terracing at Hillsborough was too be closed for that period leaving the terraces empty for the visits of Q.P.R, Watford, Blackburn Rovers and Cardiff City. Tommy was gutted. No away game until the Owls visited Newcastle United on the 15th of November. but that was going to sort out the men from the boys. That was quickly followed by Chelsea and West Ham and then it was Christmas. The boys had organised to take the Inter City Owl to Newcastle and when the lads met in Pond Street Tommy noticed the same old familiar faces were in attendance. They were met by a large police presence outside the ground and were quickly herded towards the visitors section. The Geordies seemed to be pissed off that Wednesday had brought a fair following and were chomping at the bit to get at them. As for the game Wednesday lost 1-0 and the boys grouped together to make their way back to the train. Fighting soon erupted outside the ground and the lads were handling the Geordie boys because, as always, they stuck together like glue. It was some of the best fighting Tommy had witnessed for a long time and the Owls had not been disgraced against overwhelming odds. The boys travelled straight home and finished such an enjoyable day off in the Limit.

Wednesday were doing all right, considering it was their first season in Division Two, and Tommy was loving every minute of it. Next up for the lads was a visit to Chelsea and, once again, Vinnie was providing the transport, but this time the boys were parking at Victoria and heading for the game on the tube as they were staying in London until twelve. The tube was a risky form of transportation because you never knew who you'd bump into under the streets of London. Tommy was adamant that the boys would be all right, because they were a good team and had been together now a few years and had never let one another down, even though they'd tasted one or two defeats.

Willie hated London and all the arrogant Cockneys and he was determined to send a few to sleep today. The boys emerged at the infamous Fulham Broadway station to be met by the hostile natives. But the boys just moved off in the direction of the ground and, apart from the odd insult, Chelsea did nothing. Wednesday had brought another large following and the boys settled in a pub close to the ground. Tommy could not believe that they'd not encountered any bother at the Tube, and had just been allowed on their way.

Wednesday were on the open end opposite the Shed where Tommy and his granddad had been all those years ago. Chelsea had infiltrated the Wednesday end and fighting was breaking out at the top of the terracing, but the Owls fans were soon sending the Cockneys in retreat. Inside the ground the fighting soon subsided and Wednesday suffered another defeat going down 2-0. The lads grouped together and made it outside the ground to be met by a howling mob of Chelsea supporters. Tommy thought that it would be a miracle if they ever made it to the tube. Most of the Wednesday fans were heading in the opposite direction away from the tube towards the coaches. The boys had to make a quick decision: should they head to the coach park and head back to the tube later, or make for the tube straight away and take their chance with the mob of Chelsea supporters. The boys at the front made the decision for them and headed off to the tube. Fighting soon broke out and the boys were really up against it. Chelsea were coming from everywhere and engaging the boys. The lads were fighting back best they could, but Tommy and the boys were totally outnumbered and were taking heavy casualties. The Police moved in and penned the boys into one section of the station and were having trouble keeping the mob at bay. Billy was badly cut and so was Vinnie. Macca and the rest would be bruised for weeks, but they'd done it, they'd survived the best Chelsea could throw at them.

Eventually the Police managed to send the boys on their way and the atmosphere changed from one of being very downbeat to one of joy and laughter. Tommy thought to himself what would Granddad had made of all this mindless violence that his Grandson was involved in, and Tommy quickly knew the answer. He'd have given him a good clip round the ear and told him how stupid he was.

The lads looked a sorry bunch as they made their way home early Sunday morning. Next up was a visit to West Ham in two weeks time. Tommy's mother gave him another ear bashing over Sunday dinner about his loutish behaviour and Dad was just shaking his head. The visit to West Ham had soon arrived and the boys had decided to travel by the Inter City Owl. The authorities had laid on a special tube train to Barking Station, but the boys knew it was still a long walk from the Station to Upton Park, so West Ham would have ample opportunities to engage the Owls. The lads marched off the train and headed straight for the ground. The Londoners once again put out the welcome mat with a hail of bottles and pots coming from the direction of their pub. The Police quickly forced the mob back inside the boozer and Brent said "Fancy going in there for one boys?" On the opposite corner to the Visitors End outside the ground Tommy saw a couple of lads from the days with Sham and walked across to acknowledge them, only to be told that it was football today and Tommy and his mates were fair game. Tommy knew that these West Ham fans were the business because he had seen them in action on numerous occasions while in their company following Sham. The cockneys told Tommy to be careful because after the game West Ham had got a reception committee waiting for the Owls on their long walk back to the train.

Wednesday had once again brought a good following and were herded into a section behind the goal. Insults were exchanged between the rival sets of supporters, but no violence occurred and, as for the match, Wednesday lost 2-1. Outside the ground West Ham had tried desperately to break through the police lines and engage the departing Wednesdayites, but were not having much luck. The boys were taunting them to come and get them but the police were well in control of the situation. West Ham supporters were now beckoning the Owls fans to engage them down the side streets, but it was their manor and if they wanted confrontation they would have to come and get it, just like Newcastle and Chelsea had done.

The lads were finding it a little boring that the Hammers had not engaged them all day, apart from the bottle and pot-throwing episode before the game. Then just has the boys were reaching the station it finally happened. The lads had finally got to grips with a reasonable sized mob of West Ham fans and were slugging it out like fairground prize fighters. Tommy was loving it. He was actually brawling with another London club and this time, unlike Chelsea, the lads were doing fine. To be fair to West Ham, unlike Chelsea they had not got enough numbers together to worry the very large following that Wednesday had brought on the train.

It was fast approaching Christmas and the Owls were doing fine. They had picked up 26 points before the Boxing Day game at home to Shrewsbury. On the music scene Sham had long since gone and had been replaced by the Cockney Rejects, with Tommy's saviour, from that night outside the Roxy, former Sham roadie Vince in the line up. The Clash were growing ever stronger with some excellent material. The Undertones were fast becoming one of Tommy's favourite groups and the Two-Tone scene was as strong. Tommy was still doing O.K on the job front but his love life was non-existent. On Christmas Eve the boys went into the Harrow instead of the usual jaunt into town. As the boys were in full swing a group of girls caught the lads eyes, probably because they were all dressed as naughty schoolgirls and were all wearing stockings and suspenders. Tommy was drooling into his beer and Billy was taking the piss out of him because he would not stop staring at the girls all night. "Go and chat to them. They wont bite" Billy informed Tommy. Tommy finally picked up the courage to engage the girls in conversation. "Not seen you lot in here before" he stated nervously. "We normally only go in the New Inn. We were told it was a bit rough in here" said one of them. Tommy told them that was years ago when it had a reputation for fighting every weekend, but rarely was there any trouble these days. Tommy asked where they were heading later only to be told jokingly to mind his own business. The lads said farewell to the girls and headed back to the Royal to finish the evening off.

Christmas and the New Year had been and gone and Wednesday had been dumped out of the F.A. Cup by Newcastle United. Next up for the boys was a visit to Hillsborough by Chelsea. The lads once again met in town and now had made the Old Blue Bell their meeting place. Just before 1pm a small group of very trendy looking boys walked into the pub. Tommy knew from the off that they were Chelsea supporters and that they would be well tooled up. The boys were a bit thin on the ground in the tool department but were determined to have a go if Chelsea started anything, but the lads from London just finished their beer and left. The lads got to Hillsborough and entered the East Bank to be told that all the action had happened around the ground before the game and that they had missed it.

Wednesday and Chelsea fought out a goalless draw to the disappointment of the vast majority of the 25,113 present. After the game the boys grouped on Penistone Road and awaited the arrival of the departing Londoners. Chelsea came steaming down from the Leppings Lane end and the incredible noise that they were making soon had a few Wednesdayites on their toes. Wednesday had still got a fair mob together and were having a good go at the Chelsea fans. Tommy and the boys were in the thick of things along with all the other Wednesday hooligans, but these Cockneys were well organised and they brought a formidable force up the M1. Soon the not so brave were legging it in the direction of the City leaving the rest trying to stop themselves from being slaughtered. Chelsea were now well on top and Tommy was disappearing under an avalanche of boots and fists, and fighting desperately to stay on his feet. Wednesday were in total disarray and the boys had lost control of the situation. Chelsea were advancing at great speed and totalling anyone who stood in their way. By the time the boys had re-grouped

151

themselves they were fighting a losing battle. The Londoners were in full control as the warring factions headed into town. The boys got together with what remained of the Wednesday hooligans and decided on one last go at the Londoners as they made their way to the railway station. The lads numbered no more than 30 when they confronted the Chelsea supporters in Pond Street, but they were once again totally out gunned. However, they had shown courage against an overwhelming enemy and had returned to the Blue Bell to lick their wounds. Everyone present had commented that Chelsea were the finest force for a long time to visit Hillsborough.

Tommy was once again in a bit of a state as the family sat together for their Sunday Dinner and, as usual, he was getting grief from mother about his loutish behaviour. Her words were finally beginning to sink in as he carefully got ready to go out Sunday night. Tommy had been at this game for over five years now and he wasn't getting any younger. A lot of the lads had all ready called it a day and retired from the scene all together. Out of all his mates only Billy, Bob, Chas, Ray, Shess and Gaz went on a regular basis, along with Macca, Willie, Brent and Drum from the town boys.

Tommy had organised with Webbo to take the Transit to Bristol City and the lads knew that Bristol could be a naughty place if you were caught off guard. The journey down was a nightmare as the Transit, as always, was crowded and with Friday night's leftovers filling what fresh air there was to be had, everyone was choking. The lads had all ready made two pub stops before they reached the ground and there was little or no trouble in and around the ground. Wednesday again had brought a fair following and had once again been beaten. Tommy and the boys walked back to the Transit through a park only to be confronted by a small mob of City fans, one of whom was carrying a crash helmet. Tommy and the boys, even though only numbering twelve, were well tooled for the occasion. The lads went at it toe to toe with the opposition and Willie was making good use of his trusty companion, and Macca, Brent and Drum were, as always, at Willie's side. Tommy, Billy, Bob, Chas, Gaz and Ray were once again giving it their best shot and were soon seeing off the City rabble. Webbo, Shess and Trevor had missed all the fun and were well pissed off as the happy bunch boarded the bus for the journey home.

The lads arrived home late on Saturday night and Tommy decided to give the Limit a miss because he wanted to save the remainder of what money he had left for the Harrow on Sunday night. The boys hit the Harrow about 8pm on Sunday and took up residence in their usual corner at the side of the coat stand, where they kept all the smuggled in spirits away from the prying eyes of the landlord. Tommy was well on his way when this young lady approached him with her hands laden with drinks and, in a polite manner, said "Excuse me." Tommy turned to the young lady and abruptly told her to walk round and not to disturb them again. The girl disappeared as quickly as she could in the opposite direction. Tommy was deep in conversation with the lads when a very sharp finger nail was thrust under his chin. "Don't you be so rude to my friend" said a very irate female. "Havn't you got any manners? You stand in this corner as though you own the place" she blasted at Tom. Tommy looked down at her and for once in his life was speechless. "Sorry luv, but it's been a bad day at the office so please accept my apology" said Tommy. Bob intervened and told the ladies that the man had no manners and he would give him a good taking to later on. Bob introduced the lads to the ladies. "This is Billy, Chas, Ray, Gaz, oh! and not forgetting the gobshite one who is Tommy. And my name is Bob" he said. The girl introduced her friends. She told the lads that her name was Clare and that the others were Anna, Julie, Josie, Kathy and Tanya. Tommy was ordered to the bar to buy the ladies a drink to make up for his rude behaviour. Clare and Julie were ardent Wednesday fans and had told the boys that they had left Hillsborough on the first day of the season before Half-Time because of all the trouble. Clare had told the boys that she went to the odd away game with her boyfriend and Julie. Tommy told the girls, now he was back on speaking terms, that they got into the odd scrape at the occasional game. Clare told him that they knew the boys were hooligans because a friend of theirs, called Jane, had accompanied them on a trip to Wrexham. Tommy gave her a wry smile then gulped at his beer. The new-found friends said their farewells and departed into the cold night air. Tommy told the boys on the way home that he didn't think they liked him. "Can you blame them with the way you treated the young girl?" Bob said. Tommy eventually arrived home just after midnight and slumped into bed.

Wednesday were now on a roll and by the time they'd played Derby at home the Owls were unbeaten in five games. Tommy and the boys headed straight for the Royal after the game because they'd started giving town a miss. The boys finally ended up in the Harrow where they bumped into Clare and her mates. "Have you been to the game today?" Tommy asked nervously. "Yes, but we deserved better than a draw" said Clare. The conversation finally turned to the Owls' forthcoming game at Blackburn on Saturday. "Are you going to the match?" Clare asked Tommy. Well I would but the lads are going on the train and I've got a phobia about the damned things. I just can't travel on them" he said Cheekily. Clare told Tommy that her boyfriend was taking her and Julie and if he wanted to he could go with them. Tommy took her up on the offer and told Bob not to book him onto the Inter City Owl because he was travelling by car. Tommy was told to be in the Red Lion by 11.30 on Saturday morning and was promptly met by Clare, her boyfriend Nigel and Julie.

The car had not even reached the M1 when Tommy was handed a can of beer. This was the only way to travel to football after all the other forms of transport Tommy had endured in his life; the Soccer Specials, Vinnie's Battle Buses, Webbo's Transit and The Inter City Owls. By the time they'd reached Blackburn Tommy had consumed one or two cans of beer and enough food to feed a small country. "How was the train journey?" he asked the boys when eventually he bumped into them. "Mind thi own business" Bob said venomously. Tommy introduced Clare's boyfriend to the boys and then the boys wandered off in search of some terrace activity. Tommy felt it only right that he should stay with his hosts for the day and let the lads wander off.

Wednesday had another off day and were soundly beaten 2-0. Tommy told Clare and Julie that the boys would be totally pissed off and that heads would roll. Tommy and his new companions finally arrived back at the Harrow and the boys gave Tommy the cold shoulder for the rest of the evening. Tommy thanked Clare and Nigel for their hospitality and made his way home.

The Owls were holding their own in this new division and, by the end of April, were well placed to finish in the top ten. Tommy was now spending more time in the Harrow and he hardly saw Macca and the boys. The music scene was deteriorating rapidly. It was the time of those New Romantics like Adam Ant, Duran Duran and Spandau Ballet, but Tommy still had the Clash and The Specials fighting his corner. On the job front it was ticking over nicely. He was never going to be mega rich doing what he was doing, but it still bought his beer and took him to football. As for the boys most of them had now got new interests like women and Tommy was feeling rather isolated. The boys still went to football together but in the week Tommy hardly saw Billy, Chas, Bob and Ray, unless there was a match that is. The boys sat in the Royal just before the trip to Wrexham and they were saying that it was about time that they moved away from the hostilities and concentrated on just having a good laugh like they did when they'd gone down to Wimbledon and then went on to visit Mick. Billy said that Vinnie was still running his buses so anyone who wanted to carry on could go with Vinnie and Macca. The lads were all in agreement that they would all put the troubles behind them and join the anorak and scarf brigade. Tommy made a special effort to go and see Macca and the boys to tell them that the boys had decided to call it a day. It was very rare that Tommy saw the lads these days anyway.

On the day of the Wrexham game Bob got Webbo to take them in the Transit. The day was just one big carnival and the boys were totally smashed by the time they'd got home, due to the fact Wednesday had been thrashed 4-0. Sunday night in the Harrow Clare asked Tommy if the boys fancied going to Shrewsbury Easter Tuesday, and if they'd like to share a mini-bus with them. Tommy told the lads and Billy, Bob, Chas, Gaz, Ray and Little Andy who worked with Tommy would be taking them up on their offer. Clare had got a driver and with two lads from the Lion plus Anna, Julie, Tanya and Kathy the bus was full.

On the day of the game the bus picked the boys up outside the Fairway and, before the boys had even set foot on the bus, Anna was insisting that they emptied their pockets, because the previous night in the Lion they'd been talking to one of the regulars that used to go on Charlies Coaches a few years ago and when the girls had mentioned who they were taking to the match he said "You'd better search them first because there bound to be tooled up." Tommy just laughed as he emptied his pockets, Billy was worse for wear because he'd been on the piss all day Easter Monday and Bob was eyeing up all the food and cans of booze. The idea was to spend the day in Telford then go onto Shrewsbury for the evening kick off. Tommy couldn't believe it. This was even better than his jaunt to Blackburn in the car. The beer was flowing as the Wednesdayites wended their way through the countryside. The driver had decided to take the scenic route and stop off at the odd country pub. The boys were loving this and, to be quite honest, so were the girls. The boys had been on their best behaviour all day. Anna was saying that the man in the Lion must have got the lads mixed up with somebody else, because they'd all acted like gentlemen. The party spent all the day in Telford and by the time they'd got to the match they'd all had a right skin full. Wednesday went and spoilt what had been such an enjoyable day out by getting beaten 2-0. As the boys were dropped off outside the Royal the lads thanked the ladies for such an enjoyable day.

The last game of the season saw West Ham visit Hillsborough and Tommy knew that the boys who followed Sham would be visiting Sheffield. He had gone to the game with Clare and, after seeing the Owls lose 1-0, he actually bumped into the Cockney's in Pond Street. This time they chatted to Tommy, not like that day when the boys visited Upton Park and Tommy was fair game. Wednesday finished off the season with four straight defeats and Tommy was looking forward to his first ever trouble free season when the Owls would be back in action come August.

Back in line for a trouble free season 1981 - 1982

The summer of 1981 saw the boys embark on another sortie onto foreign soil. They had booked 10 days in Majorca with the 18-30 Club. Tommy, Billy, Bob, Chas, Ian, Steve, Ray and Gaz were looking forward to having a nice rest after such an eventful season. The boys were quite pleased with the way Wednesday had adapted to life in the Second Division, finishing a credible 10th. Alan, Kevin, Neil, Geoff and Nick just wanted to forget about life down the Lane, and Dazza, Johnny and Stuart just wanted to get blitzed. Tommy had scrimped and saved like mad for these 10 days in the sun. The flight and the travelling had taken its toll on the boys and when they finally arrived they were completely knackered. They surveyed their home for the next 10 days and it seemed O.K! The rep for the company was trying his best to sell the boys his package of entertainment for their stay. Billy was trying to tell the man that only four excursions appealed to the boys and everyone of them involved drinking. So the man gave up for the time being. He asked if anybody was celebrating a birthday while they were there and Billy replied that it was his in two days time. The man ordered the waiter to bring a bottle of champagne for Billy and he proceeded to down it in one, to the man's surprise. He told the hysterical band of boys that the idea was to share it out.

With the fun over the boys went in search of the local watering holes and found quite a few. Back at the hotel the boys settled down to their evening meal and waited in anticipation for the culinary delights, and the Spanish did not disappoint. It looked like pig swill. The rep informed the boys that the first night's excursion was entirely free of charge and they were heading for Jack's bar just outside Palma. The lads were quickly on the piss and it was not long before everyone was totally smashed. The rep got everyone together and it was off to the nightclub to sample more alcohol before heading back to the hotel. Tommy was thinking that by the time they went home the boys would be raving alcoholics. On the coach Gaz noticed Johnny was missing and Chas added that he'd not seen him since they'd left Jack's. Tommy thought at this rate he'd be on his own by the time he went home. The coach headed on back to hotel minus Johnny.

Next morning as the boys lounged by the pool up the street strolled Johnny as large as life. "Where the hell's tha been?" blasted Billy. Johnny informed the boys that he'd been for a piss in Jack's and when he'd come out the coach was disappearing into the distance. He had decided that as he was on an island he would eventually finish up in Arenal, so he set off walking through the night. "Why didn't you get a taxi?" asked Tommy. Johnny replied "Because they would have fucking ripped me off, the bastards."

Tommy surveyed Sheffield's ambassadors to Spain and they looked a sorry sight. Bob enquired if anyone fancied a game of Jack's. Five lads from Leamington Spa asked what was Jack's so Tommy explained that the cards were dealt out and whoever got the first Jack picked any drink at all from behind the bar. The second Jack paid for it the third fetched it and the final Jack supped it. Tommy informed the boys that you could pick a shitty drink and finish up having to drink it. The Leamington lads joined the fun and the game began. Billy glanced at his watch and noticed it was only 11.30. "It's gonna be a long day" he said. The game started off, as always, pretty timid then, once the spirits were out in force, the game spiralled out of control. Bob loved this game because his stomach must have been made out of concrete. The game was well into its third hour and Tommy was still sober, thankfully. The stakes were soon raised and it was not long before the triple vodkas and gin were out in force. Billy couldn't believe it was nearly four o'clock and they were still going strong. The boys from Leamington were still at it, but Ray was having a bad run with the cards and looked totally smashed.

The game finally ended at five and the boys trooped off to get ready for their second night on the piss. The rep had nothing planned so the boys just hit all the local bars and finished up in some grotty nightclub where they paid an admission fee and the drinks were free all night. Ray got involved in a dispute with the club's bouncers and was quickly shown the door, quickly followed by Alan who was dragging a seven foot plastic tree out of the club to everyone's amazement. Tommy and Billy were taking the piss out of some Swedish lads and kept spilling beer on their jazzy white suits. The boys were totally out of control by the time they'd been shown the door. Bob was complaining about the bouncers being heavy handed and the boys should go back and sort them out, but Tommy explained that they were on holiday for fun not fighting so let it be.

The boys looked like shit the next morning and the rep had planned for them to go to a beach party and, seeing it had all ready been paid for, nobody wanted to give it a miss. So the lads were soon ready and off to the days festivities. On arriving at the beach the boys headed straight for the beer to be told it was only wine and sangria that was free, and this really pissed them off. Tommy was handed a plastic beaker and, as wine was not his favourite tipple, headed for the sangria. The boys just hung around the four foot tall beaker and attempted to drink it dry, but they were getting nowhere fast until Alan asked to be dipped in the sangria head first. The boys soon had a queue of eager punters who wanted to be dropped into the pot and the party degenerated at an alarming rate. The rep was none too pleased with the boys' behaviour but Tommy told him that the boys felt that they had been ripped off.

The holiday was now in full swing and the boys were constantly drunk. Tommy was really enjoying the break and with more outings on the horizon the boys were on top form. The lads from Leamington had become quite friendly with the lads from Sheffield, and so had some lads from Hatfield, just outside London. The boys just spent the days chilling round the pool but every night they would be on the piss. Next up for the boys was a trip to the Bullfight but the lads were only interested in the booze that was on offer. The barrels of wine were being given a right seeing too and the Spanish were a bit pissed off since the lads had left the tap running and they were just stood round it filling up their glasses without spilling a drop. This did not go down too well and, before they knew it, the bastards had come and confiscated the damn thing.

As the holiday wore on the food didn't get any better in the hotel. Most of the boys lived on a diet of booze and more booze. The following evening the rep had organised to take the boys to a medieval banquet and one of the Cockneys, who was in the hotel, was that pissed off with his mates hogging the bathroom that he decided to wash himself down in the sink. Unfortunately for him the sink collapsed sending water cascading out of their room and out over the balcony. Quick as a flash he was down stairs bollock naked having a shower in full view of everybody. The boys were hysterical but the hotel owners were doing their nuts. Finally the boys were on the bus heading for the banquet. When they arrived the place was massive and the 18-30 crew were shunted into the far corner out of everyone's way. The wine was brought to the table and when you'd finished the bottle they'd bring you another and take the empty one away. Tommy was getting a bit pissed off because they'd been in the place an hour and had not yet received any food, while all the other holiday makers were tucking into what looked like a feast. Billy said that the tables to the lads' right were full of Germans and they'd got the best of everything, first to get the wine and first to get the food.

When the meal was over the lads passed the word around that everybody was to save their ice cream that came in a little tub. The boys stood up and hurled the ice cream in the direction of the arrogant Germans. It was now raining ice cream to everyone's delight except for the damn Krauts.

Before everyone knew it the holiday was over and it was back to reality. Tommy was soon back at work looking forward to the brand new football season and Wednesday were away to Blackburn on the first day. Mort had once again hired a box van to take them to the match and the boys were really looking forward to their trip to Lancashire. Tommy was disappointed that Macca, Willie and Brent and his mates no longer travelled with the boys, but Tommy knew they'd be in safe hands with Vinnie. Tommy and the boys just enjoyed the comfort of the box van and the drinking before and after the game, and trouble was a thing of the past. However, if trouble arose the lads would meet it head on.

The lads were outside the Royal waiting for Mort. There were still the same old familiar faces, Billy, Bob, Ray, Chas, Gaz, Mick, who was back in Sheffield, Shess, Terry, Trevor, Chris and not forgetting Little Andy. The trip to Blackburn was an enjoyable one. Tommy thought the Owls would do well this season and they did not let the boys down in the first game, winning 1-0 to the delight of the travelling thousands.

On the way back it was a glorious sunny evening and the boys had the back of the box van open. If Mort knew about that he would be furious because it was his licence that was on the line. The lads had arranged to take the van to Luton and on the way pick up the boys from Leamington Spa. After the game the party were going to visit the lads from Hatfield and have an unofficial 18-30 reunion.

Wednesday had won their first three games of the season as the boys headed for Luton and Esso had joined them having decided to give the Lane a miss. The boys set off in plenty of time and, once again, the landlords garden furniture was put to good use. Once the lads from Leamington were safely on board the boys hit Luton just after dinner. Tommy and the boys located a nice friendly boozer and enjoyed going over the highlights of their 10 days in the sun. The five lads from Leamington were just like the boys. They enjoyed their football and enjoyed just having a good time.

Wednesday were once again awesome and sent the lads on their way to Hatfield with a 3-0 victory under their belts thus taking the Owls to the top of the league. Mort made good time and the boys were in Hatfield just after six where they headed straight for their local. Tommy was really loving this new way to do football, having all his mates with him and not getting involved in any terrace activities, but he still missed the company of Macca and the lads and Vinnie and his motley crew. But he was not missing the violence that went with it.

Tommy was once again on the pool table being, as ever, soundly beaten. Billy asked the boys from Hatfield if there was anywhere in the town with a bit of life. He was not wanting to sound disrespectful but said "Your local is as bad as ours." The boys from Hatfield totally agreed with Billy and told the lads about the White Hart, a disco pub, but it had a naughty reputation. Tommy informed the boys that they had just come

164

for a good time and trouble had not even entered into it. All the boys jumped into the van and headed for the White Hart. The place was buzzing when the boys walked in the door and a few of the locals acknowledged the their mates from Hatfield. Tommy thought that if all the boys stood together with the boys from Hatfield and didn't get too noisy they would be all right. Billy commented that it was a lively place and that he could get used to coming here of a Saturday evening.

Chas came shouting that the Owls were on Match of the Day and they had a television in the tap-room. Tommy and the boys plus the lads from Leamington and Hatfield entered the tap-room where the lads were cheering the Owls onto victory. A small number of youths sat glumly in the corner, probably a bit pissed off that some Northern bastards were having a good time in their boozer. Tommy kept a watchful eye on the miserable set in the corner and was hoping that this enjoyable evening didn't end in an all mighty punch up. Tommy pulled one of the Hatfield boys to one side and asked about the brothers grim in the corner. He was told that they were Arsenal fans and were known to cause the odd skirmish. Tommy just laughed and commented that Arsenal had a fearsome reputation up North that rivalled Leyton Orient, and with that carried on watching the Owls slaughter Luton.

Just as the landlord called last orders Mort came up to Tommy "Come and look at the van" he said. Tommy and Mort headed for the car park to survey the damage. Three of the tyres had been slashed and the van was going nowhere. Tommy told Mort to fetch Billy and Bob but not to tell the others and to get one of the Hatfield boys out here. Luckily for the boys the van was parked away from the pub so they could use it for cover if the bottles and pots started flying. Tommy knew whoever had done this wanted the boys out here in the wide open spaces. The lads had two options: they could move off and head for their mate's local or they could stay close to the van and hope it was just some mindless vandal. Billy was none too pleased when he clocked the state of the van and by now all the boys were out of the boozer. Tommy told the boys from Hatfield that if it kicked off they were not to get involved. It was the boys from Sheffield that they wanted.

Ray was busy breaking up the landlord's best bit of garden furniture and Tommy surveyed the sorry looking bunch that had been on the piss all day. He told Little Andy to get in the back of the van and stay there. Then it happened. The sour faced bastards that had been sat in the corner were leading a howling mob towards the boys. Tommy wished he'd got one of Willies spanners with him, but a table leg would have to do. Tommy and Esso charged at the Arsenal fans and, with all his might, Tommy sent the leg smashing into the scumbag's face nearly taking it off his shoulders. Billy and Bob were at it like never before. Ray was going hell for leather and the rest of the boys had quickly sobered up. The lads had actually done them, it was unbelievable. "What shall we do with the weapons?" asked Ray. "Just throw them in the van. The coppers are bound to be on their way" said Bob. Bob had spoken too soon and the Arsenal fans were having another go. With the tools in the back of the van Tommy just went for it and, with fists and boots flying, he was giving it his best shot. Just then he felt an almighty blow to the side of the head that sent him crashing to the floor. Esso could see his mate was in trouble and quickly flew at the howling mob and did some extreme damage with his lump of wood. He shouted to the boys to get Tommy back into the van because blood was pouring out of the split in his skull. Tommy was in a daze. He was not only bleeding like a good un but he was throwing up for England.

The police finally arrived when it was all over and Tommy was carted off to hospital, along with Chas and a couple of the Arsenal supporters. Mort went along with his pal and did his duty in the back of the ambulance with the sick bucket. Chas had just got a cut on the back of his head but Tommy was seriously injured. The doctors told Mort that they would be x-raying him and keeping him in overnight. Chas and Mort collected Chris, who'd had a couple of stitches, and headed back to the house in which they were staying for the evening.

As Mort walked through the door he was immediately asked about Tommy. He told the boys exactly what the doctor had said. Just then a copper called at the house and asked if anyone would like to come to the station to make a statement because they had made a couple of arrests in connection with the assault on Tommy. Bob, Chas and Gaz went along with the copper but they knew nobody saw who belted Tommy, but they would just go through the motions.

As they were sitting in the nick in walked Steve. He had pulled a bird in the White Hart and finished up in this club where the tart had given him the elbow, leaving him stranded in the middle of nowhere. So he had gone to the local railway station and unsuccessfully tried to get a train home. When that failed he got a taxi to the cop shop in the hope that they would put him up for the night.As soon as he told the copper he was from Sheffield he told him to join the lads in the other room. Esso was sporting the biggest shiner the boys had ever seen but his actions saved Tommy from even more damage than he had already suffered.

Tommy awoke the following morning to find himself fastened to a drip and he had a banging headache. The doctor informed him that he had suffered a fractured skull and had received 28 stitches in his head wound. "Where am I?" he asked the doctor. "The Queen Elizabeth in Welwyn Garden City" the doctor replied. Just after the doctor had left the boys walked in and Tommy thought he was dreaming. "What you lot doing here?" he asked. "We've come to pick you up and take you home" said Esso. Tommy told the boys the news that they were keeping him in for a few days so he asked Bob to tell his mother where he was when they got home. He also asked Billy to lend him £20 in case he had to get the train home later in the week.

The lads left Tommy in peace and made a swift exit because the nurse was giving them grief for disturbing the other patients. Tommy lay in his bed reflecting on what had started as such an enjoyable day out had turned into a full-scale battle and with only four games played in, what was supposed to be now, a trouble free season he had received such an horrendous injury.

The police visited Tommy but he could not tell them anything about his attacker and if he could he'd probably not grass him up. Tommy spent a week in hospital and because he was so far from Sheffield visiting was out of the question. On the following Friday Tommy phoned Mort to tell him that Clare had lent Tommy her season ticket and he was supposed to be meeting her in the Gate before the Derby County game, so could he drop it off to her tonight and explain the situation. Mort collected the ticket and dropped it off but there was nobody home, so he posted it through the letter box. When Clare had returned from her holiday late Friday night she had gone straight to bed and, when her mother had awoken her the first thing, she told her somebody had posted her season ticket through the door. "I can't believe it. I've lent him my season ticket and he can't be bothered to meet me in the pub for a drink, the ungrateful get" she told her mother.

It was now Saturday morning and Tommy was having his stitches removed and he asked the nurse if there was any chance of him going home. "You'll have to ask the doctor when he does his rounds" she said. Tommy spent most of the day in bed but managed to get to the T.V. room to see the football results. Wednesday had drawn 1-1 with Derby County and the lads would all be going to Barnsley on Tuesday night without Tommy. Wednesday were also away at Grimsby on the following Monday and Tommy was stuck in bloody Welwyn Garden City, by himself.

The word had soon spread around the grapevine that Tommy had been seriously hurt at a football match and probably, in some quarters, they were saying he probably deserved it. Clare was telling Anna how awful she felt when she'd phoned to tell her the news about Tommy on Sunday morning, after she'd been slagging him off for not meeting her in the Gate for the Derby match.

Tommy was finally allowed home on the 4th of October and his dad had got one of his workmates to bring him home because the family didn't have a car. Young Danny had come along to help his big brother home. Dad looked none too pleased but, deep down, he was thankful that Tommy had survived, because a skull fracture could cause serious damage.

The family arrived home Sunday teatime and Tommy was not too bad. The phone was constantly ringing and Mort asked if he fancied coming out because the lads wanted to see him. Tommy looked at his mother, who told him not to be late home. Mort picked Tommy up and they went to the Frechey were Tommy indulged in a glass of orange. He was not used to all this affection that his mates and friends were showing him. Billy, Bob and Ray wanted to contact Vinnie and get him to organise a trip to Charlton Athletic and, after the game, call on those Gooners at the White Hart. Tommy told the lads that those days were behind them and going seeking revenge would only result in some innocent punter getting a good kicking and it could be one of the boys from Hatfield.

Tommy was still off work and was spending most of his time just lazing about the house. He told his mother that Bob, Steve and Dazza were taking him to Blackburn on Wednesday night to see the Owls in the League Cup. She was a bit apprehensive, but knew that she couldn't keep him wrapped up in cotton wool. Tommy was still on the medication so a beer was out of the question, but watching the Owls was the only tonic Tommy needed and the lads came away with a 1-1 draw.

Tommy and Clare were now becoming more than friends and by the end of October were going out together. Wednesday were on top form by the end of the 1981-82 season and had finished 4th in the Second Division.

Another 20 years
of tears and joy
1982 - 2002

The Start of the 1982-83 season was to be Tommy's last as a single man, because he and Clare had decided to get married in July 1983. Most of the old school had all gone their separate ways but Billy, Bob and Chas would meet up with Tommy on match days to have a drink and talk about the old days. Tommy would occasionally bump into Macca and the lads who were still active on the violence front along with Vinnie and his happy bunch. Wednesday were having a tremendous resurgence under the leadership of Jack Charlton, Tommy was saving like mad for the big day and the away games were a bit thin on the ground. Clare was also a season ticket holder and money was really tight and, during the 1982-83 season, they only managed a couple of away trips. Billy and the boys still went on a regular basis, visiting most of the happy hunting grounds of years gone by.

Wednesday finished the season in sixth place, with the added bonus of a trip to Highbury for the F.A CUP Semi Final where they were to meet Brighton. Tommy had broken his ankle playing football and was up to his knee in plaster. It was a struggle for him to get about but he still managed a couple of beers before the game. Tommy couldn't believe he was actually watching the Owls in the semis of the Cup after the disappointment of 1966 when his dad and Uncle Don let him down. The atmosphere was tremendous and Tommy and Clare were soaking up the occasion. Wednesday played well below par and lost the game 2-1. Clare was in tears as the two of them trudged back to the coach and Tommy's foot was like a balloon. Wednesday just missed out on promotion, finishing in the top six and, to put a dampener on another miserable season, Tommy and Clare were like drowned rats as they walked away from Hillsborough after losing to Q.P.R.

The following season, 1983-84, saw Jack Charlton leave to be replaced by Howard Wilkinson. Tommy was disappointed because he liked the big man and also Bob's mum had got him to sign a wedding card for Tommy and Clare. But what a season it turned out to be after all the heartaches of all the years in the doldrums. Wednesday were back in the big time and Tommy was gutted that he was only able to make the odd away game, but with a mortgage to pay for his beloved Wednesday was tearing him apart.

The rest of the lads never missed a game that season, but they could afford it. The pair of them did manage to witness a great Wednesday victory at Cardiff. Despite that great result at Cardiff the Owls had to settle for the Runners Up spot.

The following season saw Wednesday go from strength to strength and finish eighth in the table. The 1985-86 season saw the Owls finish in their highest position since the year of 1960-61 when the Owls were second to the mighty Spurs. A ban on English clubs in Europe denied the Owls a taste of European football. Wednesday yet again managed the Semi-Finals of the F.A. Cup where they were to meet Everton at Villa Park. It had taken Tommy 20 years to finally get to see the Owls in the Semi's at the Villa. Wednesday were defeated yet again and Tommy was wondering whether he'd ever visit Wembley to see his beloved Owls.

The remainder of the eighties saw the Owls hang around the middle of the table. In the season 1988-89 Wednesday got off to a good start and Tommy and Clare were looking forward to an addition to the Wednesday. Faithful Howard Wilkinson left for Leeds leaving the Owls with Peter Eustace in Charge. The club was getting torn apart, to Tommy's dismay, and this was all the lad needed when he was about to become a Father for the first time.

On the 5th of November 1988 Clare missed her first home game for years because, as she was due to give birth to their first child, Tommy advised her against going to the Everton game. In the end she could have gone as their daughter, Samantha, was not born until the 23rd of November and this put an added strain on Tommy's slim resources. Tommy was over the moon. After all he'd been through, this was the proudest moment of his life. Eustace was finally sacked and replaced by Ron Atkinson, who managed to keep the Owls in the First Division.

The following season 1989-90 Tommy did not renew his season ticket but took a back seat and let Clare go to the match while he stayed home and looked after the baby. The boys from the Royal had organised a reunion for the match at Wolverhampton in the third round of the F.A. Cup and Tommy was asked to go. Clare told him to get off with the boys and enjoy himself, but to be careful. Billy was going along with Chas and Bob but it was mostly the youngsters from the George that were on the bus and they loved the stories of the good old days. The bus left the Royal with the boys and plenty of beer on board and, by the time they arrived in Wolverhampton, the boys were all well and truly pissed, including Tommy. There had been no trouble and Tommy was looking forward to watching the Owls in his first away game for a long time.

At the ground a surly copper asked the boys if they'd been drinking and when they replied they'd had a few the lads were banged up. Tommy could not believe he was being nicked for having a beer on the way to the game, but that was the charge. Tommy and the boys were having a problem coming to terms with the situation because it was ludicrous. Tommy told the boys that this would not happen if it was Rugby or Racing where at Ascot all the toff's are legless in the car park and plod let them drive off in their Range Rovers. Eventually, at 7.30pm, Tommy was let out and he immediately phoned Clare to tell her he'd been charged with having a drink on the way to the match and was to appear in court at a later date. Tommy was well gutted because the Owls had done the business while he was languishing in the cells.

Eventually the day of the trial had arrived and the lads took the same bus back to Wolverhampton, minus the drink. All thirteen of them were in the dock together and the magistrate took a dim view to Tommy and the boys' behaviour on that fateful day back in January. He told them that behaviour like theirs would not be tolerated and that he was fining them all £100 and banning them from attending football matches for six months. Tommy was furious that he was to miss football, not that he had been attending much as he was left at home most Saturdays looking after Samantha. Tommy thought to himself that after all he'd done on the violence front he was now classed as a football hooligan because the boys sank a few beers on the way to Wolves. The boys could not believe that the prosecution had actually had a police officer in the back of the van collecting the spent ring pulls from all the cans of beer. A grand total of 85 were found!

Towards the end of the 1989-90 season in which Tommy was banned from attending, Wednesday slumped and were relegated to the second division after spending six seasons in the top flight. Clare was heartbroken as she returned home from the Forest game and this was going to be one hell of a miserable summer.

The summer of 1990 saw Tommy move out of manufacturing and gain employment through a friend as a courier. The money was unbelievable but the hours were long. He would start work Monday morning and travel the length and breadth of Britain delivering anything from a small package to a large pallet. Clare hardly saw him, but it enabled them to renew their season tickets and adjust to life in the second division. Tommy liked his new job and with his ban lifted was able to watch the Owls every home game and travel with Clare to a lot of the away games. But he saved the best ones to go with the lads from the George. Billy and the boys had started to use the George because the lads in the Royal were a bit thin on the ground those days.

At Ipswich, on the opening game of the season, the Owls were tremendous and did not disappoint, winning 2-0. Then against Hull City David Hirst scored four times in the 5-1 victory. Tommy and Clare were able to go together thanks to her Mum and Dad babysitting. Under the guidance of Ron Atkinson the Owls were on top form and were steadily progressing to the latter stages of the League Cup. Tommy was able to go with the lads to Derby and Coventry in the League Cup but they were careful not to have any beer on board. Billy, Bob and Chas were the soul survivors from the seventies and early eighties and, along with Tommy, enjoyed the success that Wednesday were now enjoying.

The boys headed for Chelsea for the semi-final of the League Cup and, for once, the Owls had overcome the old enemy and the lads returned home with a two goal advantage for the second leg. Wednesday did not let the boys down and set themselves up against the mighty Manchester United. The boys had decided to make a weekend of it and Tommy had organised with a tour operator to take them to London on the Saturday and have a night out in London, then onto the game on Sunday. Tommy and Clare were really excited about their first visit to the twin towers and Billy, Bob and Chas were looking forward to giving the local pubs a right seeing to. Esso's brother, Steve, had come over from Jersey to join the festivities.

Once at the hotel the girl's headed for the shops while Tommy and the boys plus young Danny, who was now a regular at the matches, tagged along. The beer was flowing and all the boys were re-living the days gone by. Danny was matching the boys pint for pint and it reminded Tommy of his wedding day when Billy and Chas got Danny so drunk that he was sick in the paper shop Sunday morning when he went to do his paper round. Tommy was keeping a watchful eye on his younger brother, but he was old enough to look after himself. Tommy thought if he got into any bother his mother would blame him. Clare was none too pleased when the lads returned to the hotel with half an hour to spare before the coach left for their night-time excursion. Danny was put to bed and missed the evening's entertainment.

As the gang headed for Lambeth Tommy really enjoyed having all his mates around him as the night got into full swing. The place was buzzing and the organiser had done them proud with the evening's entertainment. The boys from the George were having a great night out and it was a disappointment when the landlord called time. Off they shot back to the hotel to finish off what had been a tremendous evening. Back in the bar Tommy and Chas were fooling around and Chas fell over a table full of drinks, sending them crashing to the floor. The owners of the drinks were none too pleased with the actions of Tommy and Chas and became very aggressive towards the boys. Tommy's mind was racing back to his hooligan days but, before he could raise a fist in anger, Clare was on his case like a shot. "You are not spoiling my weekend with your loutish behaviour" she said, as she waded into Tommy. Tommy was being pushed out of the room by Clare to the amusement of KC and the rest of the youngsters. "Is this the famous hooligan that us sprogs have heard all about?" laughed Steve, as Clare manhandled him out of the door. The lad knew when he was beaten.

The next morning it had all been forgotten and Tommy had apologised to those lads for spilling their beer. Chas's face was like thunder when he came down for breakfast. "What's up with thee?" asked Billy. "What's up with me? I'll tell thi what's up with me. It's his fucking brother. The bastard's thrown up all over the room and I've fucking walked through it when I went to bed last night" spouted Chas. The boys were in hysterics as Chas sat there trying to eat his breakfast. Tommy told Chas that it was the lads revenge for getting him drunk at his wedding all those years ago.

As the coach approached Wembley Tommy was in awe of the place. He thought to himself that he was actually there, watching the Owls take on Manchester United. Once inside the ground the atmosphere was electric with one half of the stadium a mass of blue and white. As for the game, it flashed by so quickly, even though the Owls were holding on to a one goal lead thanks to John Sheridan.

When Nigel Pearson lifted the trophy Tommy was filling up with tears of joy. After 27 years of watching the Owls he was witnessing the greatest moment of his Sheffield Wednesday life. Tommy had seen more downs than ups but all the heartache that had gone before was wiped out in those magnificent 90 minutes.

The rest of the 1990-91 season went flying by as the Owls regained their first division status. The boys had organised a coach for the trip to Oldham and Tommy was hoping for a more peaceful day out and not like the season of

80-81. Tommy knew he'd have Clare to contend with if he wandered back to the good old days of the seventies and eighties.

The day out was one of football and plenty of booze, but no trouble. The final home game of the season saw the couple take their two year old daughter Samantha to her first Wednesday game against Bristol City and the Owls were triumphant winning 3-1, not that Samantha was bothered. She was to busy chasing the blue and white balloons. Tommy was laden with balloons as he made for the exit after the game, only for him to bump into his old mate Vinnie, who must have wondered what these new found weapons were that Tommy was carrying. Tommy and Vinnie exchanged pleasantries before going their separate ways.

The summer of 1991 saw the Owls parade the Cup through the streets of Sheffield, only for Ron Atkinson to shock everyone by leaving to join Aston Villa. Trevor Francis became the first ever player manager of the Owls and the boys set off like a house on fire and, by Christmas, were in the top three. Tommy's job was going from strength to strength and, for once in his life, did not have any money problems. He was going to most of the away games with Billy, Bob and Chas and the rest of the boys from the George. Their favourite mode of transport was the mini-bus but the boys were very careful not to have any alcohol on board.

In the final away game of the season at Crystal Palace Wednesday needed a victory to clinch a place in Europe. The boys travelled down early and were in the boozer for 11.30. Tommy thought about all those years that him and Billy, Bob and Chas had travelled the length and breadth of the country watching the Owls and he couldn't believe they were only one victory away from qualifying for Europe. The boys from the George were in full swing. Lee, who was the organiser of most of the trips, his cousin Steve who was the baby of the group, KC , Davy B and Wiz were like human hand-grenades, but the older boys had a calming influence on them and trouble rarely raised its ugly head. By the way Tommy, Billy, Bob, Chas and Dazza were far too old for those games.

Wednesday fought out a memorable draw and, with Arsenal only drawing, the Owls had actually done it. The start of the 1992-93 season could not come quick enough for Tommy and Clare and she had given her blessing for the boy to follow the Owls into Europe.

The first division was now called the Premier League and United were once again doing battle with the Owls. The lads had organised to go to Luxembourg with the official travel club and Tommy had received a letter telling him that drink would not be tolerated on the trip, and if anyone turned up for the trip the worse for wear they would be refused entry to the coach. The boys decided to give the beer a miss and met in the Alexandra in town just before the coaches were due to leave for Dover. All the lads from the George were going including Danny, Tommy's brother. Once the boys were on the Ferry the bars were open and everyone hit the booze. So much for it being an alcohol-free trip! The boys spent the time playing cards and, as the queue for the bar was so long, the lads kept going to the duty free for the beer. Once they got back on the coach the steward told the boys that they were stopping at a Hypermarket in Calais to stock up on the duty free, but none of it was allowed on the coach. Tommy and the boys got around this by filling coke bottles with Bacardi and thus having one big party through France. Everytime the coach stopped the boys would replenish the bar and, by the time the lads hit Luxembourg, everyone was plastered.

The police in Luxembourg were not as petty as the plod from Wolverhampton and the boys were allowed to watch the game. The Owls were out of this world and, with another trip to Europe in the offing, it was turning out to be one hell of an expensive season. Tommy was grateful that he had a job to finance all his excursions.

The Owls were having one hell of a season, steadily progressing in the League and F.A. Cup. Tommy had been allowed to go to Europe once again. This time it was a trip to Germany to a play Kaiserslautern. Only Danny, Lee and Young Stevie were going with him on this trip and the boys had an added bonus on this trip because Chris, the lad from 1966 who had helped Tommy get those infamous semi-final tickets, was to be their steward on the journey. Tommy and Danny stocked up on the duty free and purchased two 24 packs of lager to see them through France and Germany.

The journey was not as bad as the trip to Luxembourg because the boys were better organised. Tommy was very grateful that he had such an understanding wife as Clare who backed him 100% on everything he did. As for the game it was electric and the atmosphere was second to none, and Tommy had never witnessed anything like it in his life.

The Owls were doing well in the league and were still going strong in both cup competitions, to the dismay of the red half of the city. This season, up to now, had cost Tommy a small fortune and he was very grateful that he had a job to finance it. The month of March saw the Owls win through to the League Cup Final, at the expense of Blackburn Rovers, and to set up the ultimate encounter with the Blades at Wembley in the Semi- Final of the F.A. Cup. As soon as Tommy heard the news that the tie had been switched from Elland Road to Wembley he phoned a bus company and booked a coach for the journey South, just in case the boys from the George had not got one organised. Tommy phoned Lee only to be told that the boy had all ready been on to his mate who had pencilled the boys in for one of his luxury coaches. Tommy cancelled his bus and on the day of the game he and Clare joined well over 70,000 Sheffielders on their pilgrimage South. The coach was top class and Tommy's mind was wondering back to the days when Webbo crammed them all in his battered old Transit and charged them a fiver for the privilege. Wednesday did not disappoint and easily outclassed United to set up another encounter with the mighty Arsenal.

Tommy had organised another weekend away for the League Cup Final and the boys from the George were once again making yet another trip to the twin towers. Tommy had bought a mate a ticket for the final, only to be let down at the last minute. However, the lad thought he'd have no problem shifting it outside the ground. Clare and the rest of the party made their way into the game leaving Tommy outside with his spare ticket. He was having great difficulty even getting face value for the damn thing. The touts were only offering a fiver for it, but Tommy wanted at least fifteen quid.

With the bloody game now underway Tommy sold his spare ticket to a fucking German tourist, of all people, for a measly twelve quid. Tommy rushed into the ground to locate Clare and the boys only to find out that he'd given the fucking Kraut the wrong ticket. Clare was sat next to the empty seat when the German sat at her side. She told the lad that he must be in the wrong seat. The German told Clare that he had bought the ticket outside the ground and promptly showed her his ticket. Tommy spent the rest of the game all on his own and was given some right stick when he returned to the coach. If that wasn't bad enough, Wednesday lost the game 2-1.

Tommy made two more visits to Wembley that season only to return dejected after Arsenal had once again put one over on his beloved Wednesday. So in the space of three seasons Tommy had been to Wembley five times and had returned home happy twice after victories over Manchester United and Sheffield United.

The following season 1993-94 saw the lads from the George attend nearly all of Wednesday's away games that season with the highlights being when the lads visited Norwich and Ipswich. On the way home they would stop off at Stamford. Lee had organised the driver for the trip and the Ipswich trip passed off without incident, but as for the visit to Stamford after the Norwich game, that was a different matter. The boys got to Stamford early evening and visited most of the pubs that they'd been in on their last visit. The youngsters were in high spirits but nothing Tommy hadn't witnessed a hundred times before. Just before closing the locals took exception to the lads' behaviour because their party piece was while one of them had his hands full of ale the others would pull his trousers down. Now the lad would be in a delicate situation. Should he drop his beer or stand there starkers and save the booze? There was only one result every time: the beer was a winner. All the boys were in hysterics as the boy stood there in all his glory, but the locals were not amused and one planted a size ten up the youngsters arse. The lads grouped together and Tommy's first reaction was to fall in with the boys. KC was at them head on, quickly followed by all the youngsters. The fighting spilled out onto the street and the locals were quickly dispatched, to the delight of Tommy, who had not even thrown a punch in anger.

The local plod were soon on the scene and one of the boys had his collar felt and was thrown in the meat wagon. The lads followed it to the local nick to enquire about the lads fete. Dazza was so pissed that he threw up all over the plod's shiny car. The copper was none too pleased as he disappeared back into the nick only to reappear with a bucket of water to swill down his pride and joy. The boy was eventually let out at 4.30 after being charged with being drunk and disorderly.

Tommy eventually arrived home at 8.30 with the biggest bunch of flowers Clare had ever seen in her life. Wednesday again had made it to the semi's of the League Cup and, after suffering a 1-0 defeat at Old Trafford, the Wednesday fans were attacked as they left the ground. Mobs of Reds were wading in to anyone in Blue and White and the lads managed to stay together. Tommy was furious that the Manc's were even attacking the older generation. Tommy and the boys fought the best they could against overwhelming odds and, deep down, he was really enjoying himself. The boys made it back to the coach and everyone seemed to be in good spirits, despite the fighting and the defeat at the hands of Manchester United.

Wednesday did not make the League Cup Final and finished 7th in the League. The season 1994-95 saw the Owls struggle and after such a dismal season Francis left the club to be replaced by David Pleat. For the start of the 1995-96 season Tommy was not impressed with the Owls' new boss and things went from bad to worse, with the Owls languishing near the foot of the table all season, eventually finishing in 15th place.

The following season, 1996-97, the Owls got off to a great start and everyone was optimistic that the Owls had once again turned the corner. Tommy was beginning to wonder if he'd been wrong about David Pleat as the Owls finished a respectable 7th in the table. 1997-98 saw the Owls make a shocking start to the campaign suffering a humiliating defeat 7-2 against Blackburn Rovers, then Derby stuffed the Owls 5-2 at Hillsborough. Wednesday sacked Pleat and Big Ron returned to steady the ship and Tommy was hoping that Atkinson would be given the job on a permanent basis. This was not to be, and Wednesday appointed Danny Wilson for the

1998-99 season. In his first season in charge Wednesday finished 12th and the future was looking bright again for Tommy and the boys. Tommy had arranged to visit his old mate Archie who was now a resident of Middlesbrough. He'd got Clare's permission to stay overnight at Archie's. Joining Tommy on this trip up North were Wiz, Davy B and Andy. The boys met Archie, and Tommy introduced him to the youngsters. The pair of them were reminiscing about the old days and that special day out at Southend all those years ago.

Archie had arranged for the lads to go to the game with the Boro' fans from his Village. A mini bus had been booked to take them to the game and the boys were soon in the pub knocking back the beer. Wednesday went and spoilt the day by getting soundly beaten, but the night was still young as the boys headed back to the boozer after the match.

Redcar was the destination for the night out and Tommy was soon a bit worse for wear. Wiz was keeping a watchful eye on the old man as he staggered around the pub. Tommy accidentally bumped into a group of youths and before he could apologize they were on his case. Wiz was soon rescuing Tommy and the pair of them felt they had overstayed their welcome. The rest of the boys made the decision to head for a curry. The meal was shite and the boys made an hasty exit without paying. Unfortunately Archie was oblivious to this and was captured by the irate owners of the curry house. The boys faced a dilemma about how best to retrieve Archie as the door was now locked and the boys had no way in. The owner insisted that they post £50 through the letterbox or he was calling the Police. The boys paid the ransom and Archie was re-united with the boys. He was none too pleased with Tommy who thought it best not to mention it to Clare when he got home. That was the last time Tommy visited his mate and days like those were now a bit thin on the ground.

The only down side about watching football these days was the ever increasing costs of the tickets that was spiralling out of control and the boys were finding it increasingly difficult to fill the buses for the away games. Tommy, Billy, Bob and Chas were now still going strong after all those years and it was well over twenty five of the bastards that the lads had spent travelling with the Owls. By the end of the 1998-99 season the Owls were still in the Premiership and everywhere they went it was those horrible plastic seats.

The 1999-2000 season saw the Owls struggle to hold onto their Premiership place and were eventually relegated back to the old second division. Things were going from bad to worse with the team being stripped of all its best players as the Owls were millions in debt. Tommy could not believe that a club, that only seven years previously had taken him into Europe twice, was languishing near the bottom of the table and at the end of the 2001-02 season just stayed out of the old third division by the skin of its teeth.

Tommy and the family were now all season ticket holders, including Samantha so it was at least affordable in the now called Nationwide League, and they were not having to pay well over £20 for a ticket to watch the Owls away from home in the Premiership. Tommy would often smile to himself when he saw the present day hooligans, with all their designer gear and their mobile phones, indulging in the terrace activities that had been transferred well away from the grounds because of those plastic seats and all the in-your-face C.C.T.V.

Tommy was reflecting on those days gone by and the activities that the boys got up to, and that the life of a hooligan would last between five and ten years. Then he would stand aside and let the next generation take over. He would still be found attending all the games, but now with his kids dispelling the myth once and for all that the hooligan is not a proper football supporter. Tommy was not a hooligan when his dad took him to his first game in 1964 or was he one when Granddad took him to Chelsea, or When the Owls were relegated on that miserable night in 1970 after losing to Manchester City. It was not until the 1974-75 season that Tommy indulged in terrace warfare when the likes of the Red Army from Old Trafford had swamped Hillsborough along with Aston Villa, who had totally invaded Hillsborough on the last game of the season by increasing the gate from just over 7,000 to a massive 23,605 in the space of five days.

By the end of the 1980-81 season he had called it a day. Tommy's days as a football hooligan had lasted him only six seasons before he fell back in line. Wednesday had nearly taken Tommy full circle from that sunny morning back in 1975, when himself, Billy, Chas and Bob set out on their epic football journey that was to last well over 25 years.

Tommy and Clare visited Stockport County on the 13th of April 2002 and witnessed another drab performance by the Owls. The team was fortunate that they were not relegated to the old Third Division, which would have really been a total disaster. Tommy had seen plenty of action during the years spent watching the Owls: all the fighting that they encountered, the arrests that the boys suffered over the years, not to mention all the injuries, including Tommy's fractured skull. Despite all that it was one thing and one thing only that saw them through all the bad times, and that was their unquestionable loyalty to one another and, most of all, their love for Sheffield Wednesday Football Club.

**